Waterside

A wonderful childhood born out of turmoil

By

David Barker

The aerial photo of the farm was taken around 1965 just before the rail track was removed

Introduction

Writing about my childhood at Waterside Farm came about primarily as a form of therapy. A way of immersing myself in happy times. I have always known how fortunate and privileged I have been to have such a happy childhood, particularly at Waterside Farm. So, the hope was that by concentrating my thoughts on recounting the events and the antics and the friends of that time and writing it down on paper would help me return to a place I had been just months before, a place that now seemed almost alien. The world I had somehow slipped into seemed all too real and impossible to escape. But I knew I could escape because I had done it before. Many years previously after slipping into the ditch at the side of the road of life, I started to write about hitch-hiking and travelling Europe with a friend of mine.

Writing is just one of many tools to help get back on track, two of the others being exercise and work, and the last time this happened work took over as I got going again.

This left my writing redundant to languish in a cupboard for evermore. However, this time we were hit with the phenomenon of lockdown which afforded me more time. So, I was able to recount all my memories of our time at Waterside Farm, which with the help of a few treasured photographs also became a small snapshot of our family history for members of the family in the future.

Acknowledgements

In helping me to have a wonderful childhood at Waterside Farm, thanks are due firstly to Mother and Father, Jenny, Alison, Steven and Richard, with others along the way being Malcolm and all the Rosses, Paul, Andrew and Stephen. And not forgetting the scout movement with the likes of Mr Wilson giving their precious time and knowledge. I would further thank Jenny for her technical support and cousin Sandra for the historical paperwork and photos.

Chapter 1

My first memory of Waterside Farm was of my dad telling me we were going to move to a farm, something I remember I wasn't too happy about, but he sold it to me by telling me that my bedroom has a window on the floor. A strange thing to say I know but it was something that really set my imagination going. A window on the floor. I just couldn't picture what that would be like. This was 1963 and I had just turned five years old, so I didn't ask Dad to elaborate. I was going to have a bedroom with a window on the floor and I couldn't wait to see it.

We lived down Jefferson Drive in Brough near Hull and I hadn't started school yet so didn't have too many friends, just a girl called Ruth and a boy called Baby Ralph, whose mother would insist on giving Ralph and me a spoonful of cod liver oil whenever I went round there. She would line us up then pinching your nose would tip this awful liquid down our throats. So, whilst Ralph was my best friend I wasn't going to miss playtime at Ralph's too much.

Our family at the time consisted of myself, two younger sisters, Mum, Dad, and a young black dog called Brandy. I don't remember too much about my sisters from that time. I guess they were too young and noisy.

Mum was quite well educated. Her mum and dad owned Hardings Fireplaces in Hull and Leeds. Dad being less educated had earnt his money at an early age from keeping and breeding pigs and rabbits in sties and sheds wherever he could find them. Grandad on my father's side had split from Nana and was a council road man at Holme upon Spalding Moor, which is where Waterside Farm was located.

Driving down the track that led to the farm was something I remember well. Large willow trees obscured the farmhouse itself, and as we pulled into the farmyard the first thing I saw was a number of chickens. They almost looked as if they were there to greet us but were I'm sure after any food that might be

3

on offer. Chickens were a creature that I had been introduced to before and had a photo somewhere with one on my knee. Chickens would become one of my favourite creatures on the farm.

The farmhouse as I remember had electricity, the kitchen had just a cold tap and there was no bathroom. There was a kitchen dining area, a living room, and if you were going to be posh a reception room. This room had about fifteen iron hooks on the ceiling so had been used for hanging meat in the past, and there was also a clothes dryer on a pulley hanging from the ceiling too. A steep set of stairs were accessed from this room through a latched door at the bottom. At the top were four bedrooms, one of which would become the bathroom in due course. Off the back door was a veranda for all the footwear and coats. The toilet was in a building at the side of the veranda, a chemical toilet with the distinctive smell of Jeyes Fluid. Also in there was a copper and a tin bath. This would have been the previous owner's bathroom and ours too for the coming weeks. Either side of the house were a couple of stables with old halters and other horse related items left by the previous owners. Outside at the back of one of the stables was an old toilet. A small door went into a little room which had a bench with two toilet seats fashioned into it, a sort of his and hers side by side with a door underneath for cleaning it out. I do remember that it hadn't been cleaned out for some years and wasn't something we ever used.

The first thing I recall on first entering the house was a distinctive smell. I guess it was an old working farmhouse smell. The next thing I noticed was the wear on the quarry tiles. There was a definite trough in the tiles going round into the kitchen, which could only be caused by millennia of footsteps. Following this trough into the well kitchen would be stretching things a bit, it just had a Belfast sink with a tap and a couple of old free-standing kitchen units. From here you turned right into the dining area, then turning right through a door at the end of the room went into a little lobby where the front door was, then through another door into the living room, and from there led back into the reception room.

Climbing the stairs for the first time was the exciting bit for me to find the room with a window on the floor which was the first room on the left. It wasn't as I had imagined. I thought it would be a window literally flat on the floor that you could somehow look outside. In fact the roof sloped down and the window went from the floor to the sloping ceiling, but in time I grew to like my window on the floor and from the comfort of my bed I would be able to see the whole of the stackyard with the roaming chickens and the passing of the steam trains beyond.

The farm itself had a fairly large barn, an old grain store at the side of a foldyard which was surrounded by a number of stables and pig sties. There was a tractor shed and a long chicken hut and a couple of lean-to buildings. Surrounding the buildings were four fields totalling about fifty acres, not a vast acreage but enough for Dad to farm by himself. At the edge of the field at the back ran the steam railway from Market Weighton to Selby, and beyond that was the river foulness which would turn out to be a popular haunt during the summer holidays.

The weeks went by as we settled into our new surroundings. Dad had things to acquire, like a grey Ferguson tractor with two slype plough, plus a drag and a trailer. He also bought an old pick-up. Mother had my sisters and myself to look after plus things to sort out around the house. It would be quite some time before the bathroom would be up and running as there was a lot of plumbing to be done, not least the installation of a septic tank. So, in the meantime the hand washing of clothes in the copper was the order of the day.

Dad had either bought or found a hand push seed drill and had begun preparing a portion of land to sow what he called cash crops. So, there was a patch where he would broadcast some radish seed and then sections where he would sow onions, beetroot, cabbage, lettuce, turnips, etc. He later borrowed a potato planter and planted a number of acres, a job I remember helping with at one point. There were two seats at the back of the planter which you sat on then took potatoes out of the hopper and dropped them down a tube when a bell rang which ensured the potatoes were spaced correctly.

It wasn't long before the pig sties were filling up with pigs ready for breeding, and more chickens were brought in to join the resident ones we already had. It was not long before the workload grew, the teething and tailing of the piglets, and the cleaning out of the pens which all had to be done by hand. Radishes would soon grow and would have to be picked into bunches. Dad had a wholesaler called Norman Williamson who would buy all our vegetable and salad produce that we had grown. I remember Mr Williamson as being a real character with a very distinctive voice who would call my dad Jos, which was actually my grandad's name, my dad's name being Gordon.

I used to enjoy our trips through to Gilberdyke with the pick-up laden with produce, Dad wrestling with the column gear change and the smells and rattles as we rumbled along.

The day had come for my first day at junior school and I wasn't happy about it at all. I was happy helping Dad where I could round the farm. I remember tearfully hanging on to Dad until he managed to prise me away with a gift of a Milky Way. I was finally taken to the class of Mrs Ansel where other children were also suffering the first day blues. I remember distinctly a girl being cleaned up behind some free-standing blackboards. But it was a relatively small class and friends were soon made, namely Malcolm Ross who lived fairly close to Waterside Farm whose father was a manager at the milk factory near the train station at the edge of the village.

It was over a mile to school so in the early days Mum would take me to school, usually in the car which at that time was an old Ford Popular. Some days Dad would have to start it with the starting handle, and when that didn't work he would tow us off with the tractor. Never a dull moment on the farm. Another milestone that came along shortly after my first school day was the day I learned to ride a bike, which was the classic "don't let go, Dad, don't let go", only to find out he had let go some time ago. The bike they had got me was too big so Dad had fastened blocks of wood to the pedals so I could pedal comfortably, which was okay but meant getting on and off was difficult. My first ride was okay as Dad helped me to get on and off, so over the coming weeks I had to develop my own method which was hit and miss for a long time. At the farm I used a big log near the willow trees to get on the bike and all manner of things as I went further afield, and to get off I had to slow down and lean the bike to one side and almost fall off.

All was going well with the bike riding until one hot day when I was riding along in just my shorts I tried to dismount while perhaps going a little too fast and ended up falling into a large bed of nettles near the trees. I was literally stung from head to foot and after many tears and Mum covering me in camomile lotion, I was sitting in the garden snivelling and feeling sorry for myself, when a boy from the neighbouring farm appeared in the long grass at the other side of the dyke that separated the properties. After a few tentative words of introduction and me telling him of my accident he duly jumped across the dyke to survey my injuries, which all of a sudden I became proud of. My whole body was covered in pimples which in many places had merged together to form large raised red patches. He had already started to tell me of his cure for nettle stings which was to cover them in dock leaves, but on closer inspection quickly decided I had far too many stings to successfully cover. The best cure for the stings in the end was our meeting. His name was Paul Simpson and would become a regular visitor to the farm and a good friend.

The growing season was rolling on and an abundance of produce was now ready, so Dad had decided not to take it all through to the wholesalers but to load up the trailer with as many different salad and vegetable items as possible and sell them on the roadside. So early one morning Dad loaded up the trailer arranging the produce in wooden trays so he could show them off. He then plonked me in the middle of the trailer before we made our way across the field to set up camp at the roadside. Once there Dad began to measure out some of the produce into paper bags using an old set of scales in anticipation of a run of customers. He had a number of signs that he had prepared, fresh veg for sale and potatoes so much a bag, which he put up about fifty yards in each direction to help bring the customers in.

When all was ready we sat and waited for the first customer and we didn't have to wait long. In fact, once someone stopped it seemed to start a constant run of customers which had Dad run off his feet and he had to instruct me to start weighing more items of veg into bags as they ran low. He didn't have a till of any kind and on this first trip he used some of his empty Park Drive cigarette packets to push the notes in. It was a little chaotic as we didn't really know what to expect. On subsequent trips though he pushed the boat out and had a long narrow tin to keep the takings in, which fascinated me because as the day wore on the tin would be wedged full of notes and coins. It was a success and something he did on a regular basis over the following weeks.

As time went by and my sisters got older, Jenny, who was just over a year younger than me, became my main playmate making dens in the straw shed for one. Dad had filled the long chicken shed with straw leaving the chickens to roost wherever they wanted which they seemed to manage quite well. The only downside to this however was that the chicken nests with eggs in could be found all over the farm. We used to love picking eggs from the popular nests that we had found and we never tired of finding fresh eggs in nests. But every now and then you would find a new nest somewhere full of eggs which would usually turn out to be not that new, and we quickly learned not to crack eggs directly into the pan. If they passed the pan of water test they were then cracked into a saucer for inspection first. Being around the chickens and finding eggs was one of our favourite jobs.

Another pastime we liked was going and watching the pigs, either suckling their mother or just running around in the fresh straw when they got older. We also liked to throw a big potato into a large sow's pen and watch it chomp away on it creating a froth round its mouth as it merrily munched away. Dad would often have us as spectators when he fed the pigs. He would get a big bucket with a bit of water in it then tip in some meal which consisted of milled barley, wheat, bran and other

8

goodies. This he then stirred with a stick into a thick porridge. Again, the best bit was to watch the pigs devour it with great noise and urgency. This was a job which in time we would be trusted to help with.

At the age of seven I learned to drive the tractor for the first time. I had climbed up and sat on the tractor many times on my own and even almost started it one time. I had seen Dad put the tractor into gear before so one time as I was pretending to drive it I pushed the gear stick and the engine turned over which frightened me a bit. To start the tractor you turned the key then pushed the gear stick to the S for start which is what I did, only I hadn't turned the key but hearing the engine suddenly turn over taught me a lesson.

My first proper drive was out in a stubble field spreading manure. Dad had loaded the trailer by hand from the pigpens then drove it out into the open field, then he got me to sit on the seat while he stood on the drawbar behind me. Then he told me to push the clutch in and put it into first gear then let the clutch out slowly. I didn't need to touch the hand throttle as we only needed to move very slowly, which was quite an easy way to get used to being in the driving seat. Once Dad was happy that I knew how to stop and turn as we were moving so slow he climbed from the drawbar into the trailer, then standing at the back of the trailer he started to spread the manure with a fork. It was hard work for Dad but absolute heaven for me. I know I was trying to look serious but inside I was absolutely bubbling over with excitement. My driving lesson however came to an abrupt end on the second load when Dad put the fork through his big toe. This was soon treated by Mum who simply put antiseptic and a bandage on and after a cup of tea and a sandwich Dad was back doing other chores leaving the rest of the muck spreading for another day.

Now that I was getting a little older Paul and myself were starting to venture a little further afield. We each had a sheaf knife fastened to our belts which were put to good use in the copse of willows down Holly Lane. Hidden in the middle of the willows we would make our first bow and arrows. I remember a number of failures but in the end we made some very effective weapons. Well, they were to us anyhow and hitting large stationary objects was a big achievement in our eyes. We had dens all over and would only go back to the farm when we got hungry.

One day while exploring the boundary hedgerows we came across a small building just on the other side of the hedge. After having a good look around the outside and being happy no animals were inside we slowly opened the door. On one side was a big built-in pig trough, on the other side was a long shelf about three feet high on top of which was about thirty, eight stone bags of fertiliser stacked up four or five high. In the middle was a scuttle, a fairly big round metal container with a handle on either side. We had a look around before one of us, and I can't honestly remember who, took out his sheaf knife and slowly pushed it into one of the bottom fertiliser bags and watched as a few grains of fertiliser trickled to the ground. We looked at each other as we wondered what to do.

There was only one thing to do: take the scuttle and put it underneath to catch the falling grains. I have to say for some reason we didn't see anything wrong in what we were doing. In fact the scuttle seemed to be filling too slow so we made the cut a little bigger and watched the scuttle slowly fill, then before it ran over we grabbed a handle each and carried the scuttle and tipped it into the trough and then put it back under to catch more. When this bag stopped running out we cut into another one and so the process went on. It became a job of work and we actually believed we had achieved something. In all we cut about four bags. A job well done is how we felt.

We soon learned the error of our ways. Just a few days later I was helping Dad on the trailer selling produce again when Ken Huddlestone, the neighbouring landowner, pulled up in his van to ask Dad if he had seen anybody messing about near his building and told Dad what he had found. Dad looked straight at me. "Do you know anything about that?"

"No, Dad," was my reply after Mr Huddlestone drove away. Dad asked me again with a knowing glare. "Yes, it was me and Paul." I spilled the beans and was promptly sent home to bed.

What was Dad like? Well, he was a six feet tall robust, balding man who would seldom be seen without his flat cap. He was hard working and had time for anyone and everyone including us of course. He would often spoil us in some way or another and Christmas was a magical time thanks to Mum and Dad. The build up to Christmas was a family affair as we sat with Mum making paper chains for Dad to hang across the ceilings and decorate the fresh spruce tree that Dad had put up. Santa Claus was kept alive with myself and Jenny sworn to secrecy when we found out the awful truth for the sake of our younger sister and brothers. We had enjoyed greatly the excitement of leaving a glass of sherry and a mince pie by the fireside on Christmas Eve, then waking on Christmas morning to find a pillowcase full of toys and fruit. I had some nice toys like Meccano, Scalextric, a train set and a donkey boiler. Dad enjoyed helping me set them up and should I say made sure I was playing with it properly, especially the Meccano. I remember him helping me for hours to make a windmill out of the Meccano then rigging up the donkey boiler to power it. They were good times. He liked to go to the pub at some point on a weekend. I know he made contacts there, sourcing people that could give him a hand at certain times for one, and he would come home with all kinds of things. One time he came home with several boxes of tins of food like steak, peas, sago and I think carrots, which he got really cheap. The reason they were cheap was because there were no labels on them. So, you can imagine Mum trying to find a tin of steak and opening two tins of sago or vice versa, which created a chuckle or two for quite some time. Whenever Dad went to the pub he would always take his mouth organ with him, and when the right time of evening and atmosphere was reached he would readily start a sing along. This would happen at home too when conditions were right.

In spite of the workload Dad still had time for some downtime and taking me fishing down to the foulness for a few hours now and then was something I looked forward to. There was always a resident pike under the bridge, a scary looking fish when you saw it close up, even scarier when Dad caught

11

one. His favourite quarry were big roach which you couldn't get close to so he would trot a line down the river with a bit of bread on. Not easy to catch which made it all the more rewarding when he did. Another fish he liked to catch was dace which he caught further down where the water was shallower. River fishing was a bit too difficult for a young first-time fisherman, so one day Dad took me to Touse's pond a few miles away, set in the middle of a field surrounded on two sides by bushes. It was here that I would catch my first fish. Dad first took two slices of bread, dipped it in the water then squeezed much of the water out and kneaded it into a stiff paste. He put me together a rod and reel showing me how to attach the float and leads then finally tying the hook on. A small piece of paste was placed over the hook and it was ready for me to cast in. The cast didn't go very far but then it didn't need to as the pond was full of roach, and in no time at all the float was bobbing about before it darted under, of course catching me off guard till Dad told me to wind it in. It was then that I felt the tug of a small roach as it darted about. Moments later I had it out of the water and laid on the bank side. A very sleek silvery-blue fish with red eyes was now unhooked by Dad before he gave it to me to put back in the water. I was quite happy holding it and took a moment to look at it before it was returned. That was the start of a lifelong passion for angling and observing nature.

Mother was a very capable person who seldom let things get on top of her, especially early on at the farm when she had to help out more. She made sure we knew the dangers around the farm and kept us entertained when the weather was bad. We had a piano which she played a bit and would teach us some of the easy pieces to play, which was quite fun. She would also play games with us from snap to rummy as we got older, some of the moments being so funny we still remember them today. She was quite resourceful and would make or make do if there was something we hadn't or couldn't afford. We always had a good breakfast and a meal round the table at teatime. We were allowed to play but also had to be responsible when Mum had other things to do. We grew up fast and were trusted with many things from an early age.

Malcolm Ross had become a good friend and I would spend many hours at his house as he did at ours. He had two brothers, Keith and Michael, which made for a good number when playing board games which we did a lot, so much so that Malcolm's mother would have to turf us outside if we had been in for too long. Malcolm's father was a manager at the milk factory which was just down the lane, so sometimes we would go down there for a mooch round. It had a snooker room which we weren't big enough to play, but it was on the second floor so it was a great place to spend some time, especially when Malcolm's dad would bring us some chocolate crumb. It was a raw product made at the factory which I had been shown before as it comes out of big ovens. Trays are set on trolleys and each slab of chocolate crumb would be about six feet by three feet and about an inch and a half thick, and Malcolm's dad would simply break a couple of chunks off for us to nibble on. It had a very distinctive smell and was usually still warm which kept us quiet for a while. It was nice.

Chapter 2

After two years at the farm my first brother was born. My sisters and I were at school when Steven was born at home. So, it was a big surprise when we got home. There were many homecoming surprises, not all new brothers of course. One day we came home to find a billy goat standing in our path. We had to run round the farmhouse with the goat in hot pursuit, shutting the veranda door moments before the goat butted it with its horns. Betty, as it was called, was from that day on penned up. I think Dad thought he would be able to let it wander freely, but as friendly as it was Betty was just too dangerous. Another addition to the farm that came soon after Steven was a pony called Brough which would receive almost as much attention as Steven. It was a very good-natured pony which was good as we didn't have a saddle to start with. With me being the eldest I would ride Brough the most initially, with Jenny and Alison needing Dad to put them on and lead them about. Later on though Jenny proved to have the greater passion for horse riding and husbandry.

On some still misty evenings or early mornings Dad would take me shooting. We would go along the railway embankment where the foulness would come close to the railway on the opposing embankment and wait for ducks to either fly on or off the foulness. More often than not he wouldn't get anything, but every now and then he would get a duck or sometimes a pheasant or partridge. These would then be plucked and prepared for cooking. Dad was an accomplished cook so would sometimes cook dinner himself.

One day Dad said we would go shooting early in the morning, something I was always excited about. I especially liked the early morning quiet and the anticipation and so was up and dressed and ready to go at six am. When Dad didn't appear I crept into Mum and Dad's bedroom to wake him. It was Mum who woke first and quickly whispered what was I doing. I just as quickly whispered back only to be told to go back to bed as

Dad must be tired. I remember being so disappointed that I couldn't get back to sleep, and then more frustrated when Dad said later that I should have woken him up.

On the back of this Dad bought me an airgun so I could go shooting when I wanted. Not for ducks and pheasants, but rabbits and rats. After initially shooting at targets I would sometimes sit in the barn to shoot rats, and then some days I would sit with Brandy near the rabbit holes on the railway embankment. After sitting there for ages a steam train would come past and Brandy would chase after it barking, so all in all my success rate wasn't that great. However, just sitting and waiting in the outdoors for hours helped me to see wildlife events that I probably wouldn't otherwise have seen. The formation of a molehill from scratch isn't something many people have seen.

I would watch lapwings land some distance from their nests and then scurry this way and that as they made their way so as to keep its location less obvious. Sometimes they would dive bomb me if I got too close to their nest and a few times I would see them feigning injury. They would limp along the ground holding their wing as if injured trying to entice you away. It was here too that I first watched a skylark take off and start to sing its song climbing higher and higher as it did so, until it reached a certain height where it would stop singing and then swoop silently down to the ground where it would repeat the whole process again. I also watched a barn owl catch a vole on the railway embankment. It is I suppose with some irony that from a wish to kill some wildlife I learned to appreciate it, and to this day it is one reason I still like to go fishing.

My Grandad Jos, my dad's father, lived in a cottage on a piece of land with his sister at the other end of the village owned by the council. He worked for the council as what I think they would call a roadsweeper back then. He would keep the village tidy and dig dykes and trenches by hand to stop flooding on the roads. He didn't drive so would always use his bicycle to get around, no helmet or fancy clothing back then, just a pair of bicycle clips to keep your trousers from getting caught in the chain. He reminds me now of Greengrass from the series *Heartbeat* as he always wore a big dark coat which would quite often have a four ten shotgun and a dead rabbit hanging from under it. There were some allotments on his way to the farm which he would often stop at and shoot a rabbit, which he would leave with us to have for dinner. I wasn't keen on eating rabbit so I was told it was chicken. However, I could see shot marks on some of the meat and sometimes a lead shot would roll across the plate as you cut into the meat. They would have got away with it perhaps if they had said it was duck.

Grandad would pop round at regular intervals throughout the year and was always a welcome sight, not least because he would always have a Nuttall's Mintoe or two in his pocket. He would get Jenny and myself to do jobs around the farm, but in a way that didn't seem like work. Like the time he got us to weed onions. First he got a hessian sack or two from the barn along with some Massey Harris which was twine that came in big spools for the straw baler. He then wrapped the hessian round our knees and tied it into place with the twine, which we found amusing. We then had to kneel down astride a row of onions each. They were spring onions about six inches high which could hardly be seen for weeds including nettles. We then had to carefully pull out the weeds while leaving the onions in place.

After some time of shuffling along and concentrating on pulling just the weeds out, I can remember turning round on my knees a bit to see this clean row of onions behind me and being amazed and pleased at the transformation. The rows were just long enough, any longer and we may have tired of the job, but at the end of the row Grandad would give us a sixpence each which of course would delight us no end. After a small break and making sure our sixpence was safe, off we would go on the next row. Our fingers when we finished were green and dirty and tingling a little from the nettles but didn't seem to matter as we sat and counted our money.

At the farm we weren't self-sufficient but not far off. There was an orchard with apples, pears and plums. Dad would butcher a pig every now and then for ham, bacon and pork. He would pluck the odd chicken with pheasant, partridge and rabbit thrown in. We of course had our own vegetables and eggs and would bake our own bread but not all the time.

I have no memory of going food shopping with Mum or Dad. Of course back then there weren't the large supermarkets we have now, so Mum would just pick up bits and pieces as we needed them. There were only a couple of shops that I remember going in and they were Hodgson's corner shop where I would get my sweets and pop, and Lumley's mobile shop. Although I liked to go to Hodgson's, Lumley's was far more exciting mainly due to them arriving out of the blue especially when they came on a winter's evening when it was dark. We could be watching the television in our pyjamas when someone would shout out "Lumley's are here" and we would run around putting on dressing gowns and Wellington boots to join Mum in the big van through the sliding door at the side. Inside was an Aladdin's cave of goodies which we would do our best to get Mum to buy, but given the time of night and Mum not caving into our every wish it would just be some small treat or biscuit along with some of the more essentials that she would buy. A few other things that went towards self-sufficiency was having a go with a butter churn which had been left by the previous owners. After first giving the churn a good clean out and with a quantity of fresh cream Dad had acquired from a local farmer, we were given the task of taking it in turns to turn the handle of the churn until the milk solidified enough to pat into blocks of butter. This I remember took quite some time leaving us with aching arms but being absolutely amazed at the magical transformation when we opened it up from the liquid cream we had first put in. However, the novelty of the process wore off in time and the butter churn was yet again returned to reside in one of the outbuildings.

Another money saving activity that Mum and Dad would do was to make their own wine and would have several demijohns on the go at any one time, wheat and barley being the most popular but they also made stranger ones like nettle and elderflower which didn't sound too appetising to us. I remember the wine never made it to the bottle stage, it would just be syphoned off into a jug to top up their glasses. Another drink they would have from time to time was QC sherry which Jenny and myself liked a lot, and some mornings after Mum and Dad had had a sherry the night before we would find a bit left in a glass near the sofa and would take it in turns to finish it off. I will still have a little QC to this day.

I enjoyed my early schooldays moving from the infant class of Mrs Ansel to Mr Asker's class. He covered quite a broad spectrum from maths and English to sport and gardening. I remember our very first football match, if you could call it that. After dividing us into two teams and showing us the positions we should all take, he told us a few basic rules and the aim of the game before blowing the whistle for start of play. Within a very short space of time we became one big huddle of boys chasing whoever was kicking the ball and making an awful lot of noise too.

Over time things sorted themselves out and it became clear who the good players were and which poor lads were picked last. Looking back having two boys picking their teams from the pack and ending up with the same boys being last every time perhaps wasn't the best system. However, football isn't everything and many would excel in other pursuits. The school had a garden with flowerbeds and a vegetable plot which everyone would help with and enjoy throughout the year. Dinnertimes were always a favourite time of day. The canteen was a separate building at the other side of the playground and as you walked across the playground to the canteen you were always hit with this distinctive smell. It was a nice smell of cooked food which never changed no matter what the menu was. Only once in my life since have I ever caught that essence to remind me of those times.

There were a number of events throughout the year that I remember fondly, one being the harvest festival which would be held in the hall. Parents of all the children would bring baskets of vegetables, fruits and salad which were positioned at the front of the hall on trestles and tables with sheaves of wheat and flowers to create a truly wonderful display. We would then sing hymns such as "we plough the fields and scatter the good seed on the land", and the produce would then be given to charitable causes.

Sports day was a day I looked forward to as well, watching David Simms the master of the sack race sticking his toes in the corner of the sack and almost running, leaving everyone else standing as they jumped along behind. I was always neck and neck at the one hundred yards with Paul Harrison, and the egg and spoon race could be anyone's as eggs fell to the ground yards from the finish. Another favourite was the nativity play at Christmas. Much time and effort was spent on the Christmas decoration with the stencilling of windows to the making of paper chains being something we all helped with. Many sprigs of holly and painted branches were hung throughout the school to give a wonderful Christmas feel. The buzz of the classroom where we fitted our costumes before we went out to perform was great fun, and perhaps being one of the shepherds with no lines to speak helped our enjoyment along. The school made good effect of the spiral staircase which came down from the head teacher's office to the hall for the angel Gabriel to appear from.

The fun continued into the intermission as we took our toilet break. The toilets were outside across the playground with the boys having a couple of toilets with latched doors and the urinals with no roof on. The week of the nativity had been cold with snow and the playground was covered in slides that had been made during the day from shuffling along to pack the snow down which turned to ice leaving long glasslike slides. The night was still and cold and the snow muffled the sound of our laughter as we came out onto the playground lit by a few dim outside lights. We all ran in different directions the three kings and the shepherds interspersed with angels sliding in all directions wishing the evening would never end.

Jenny, Alison, Dad, Ralf and Me

Grandad in pub, third from left

Mum, Jenny and myself, one of the few pictures of Mum from that time, as Mum was usually the one taking the photos.

Grandad Jos, Aunty Polly and Uncle Tony outside Boggle House. When Grandad and Aunty Polly left the house it remained empty for many years before it was finally pulled down

Uncle John, Cousin Tracey, Dad, Alison
and Jenny outside of main Barn

Dad fixing the roof above my
bedroom window on the floor

Chapter 3

My grandmother and grandad, (my mother's mum and dad), had moved into a bungalow opposite the farm. Grandad had Hardings Fireplaces in Hull and Leeds. He was a lovely man and very different from Grandad Jos. That's not to say that Grandad Jos wasn't a lovely man too. They lived very different lives and Grandad Harding had to spend a lot of time looking after my grandmother who was now blind and had other complications due to diabetes, so would only seldom call at the farm usually in their chauffeur driven Jaguar and they would always be well dressed, Grandad always in a suit. You certainly wouldn't' have caught him weeding onions!

Of course, we would usually want a ride in the Jaguar which he duly did leaving Grandma to catch up with Mum, just a run to the other end of the village and back was enough to keep us quiet. I always remember sitting behind the chauffeur. He was an elderly gentleman with a long neck which was covered in old wrinkles which were now like a network of groves which fascinated me more than the car ride. They didn't usually stay too long, just a cup of tea and a sandwich, and Grandma would catch up on things we had been doing at school and round the farm. We would tell her about the pony and Betty the goat which would make her laugh. In spite of her condition she was always laughing.

They previously lived in South Cave where we would visit from time to time, but now they lived opposite we saw more of them. Grandad would sometimes cook us tea which was almost always the same thing: stewing steak, vegetables and new potatoes. He liked gadgets, especially kitchen ones. I remember him showing me his new potato peeler which was an electric bowl with a very rough surface on the bottom and sides. He would put the clear lid on then turn it on and the new potatoes would dance around the bowl as it began to vibrate slowly removing their peel. We have a cherished photo of Grandad with all of his workers, his brother and our uncle standing in and around one of his wagons somewhere in Hull.

In the early days at the farm Dad would do the odd day or two of work for Grandad building some of Grandad's fireplaces, usually in private properties in Leeds, and would take me along with him on a few occasions. On our birthdays we would always get a card from Grandad and Grandma which would always have a five pound note in which was a lot of money then. I did get a present from them once which was two cars for my Scalextric, a green and a red MGBGT, which I cherished for a long time.

Malcolm Ross was going to join the cub scouts so I decided to join with him, something Mum and Dad were happy for me to do. Mum bought me a uniform, a green shirt with scarf and toggle and a cap, and together with a pair of school shorts I looked and felt the part. The cub scouts met in the village in a big wooden hut. I remember going on my first night with Malcolm and meeting some of the other cubs, some of whom we already knew, squatting down with two fingers of each hand on the floor and chanting, "Akala, we will do our best." We enjoyed our evenings learning all about the cub scout movement and for part of the evening we would learn how to tie knots and how to identify different flags, then we would play games like British bulldog. One boy would stand in the middle of the hut while the rest of us each with a piece of wool tied round our arms would have to get past him to the other end. If he pulled the wool off your arm you then joined him in the middle to become another bulldog. Another game was where one of us would be blindfolded and sat on a chair with a boxing glove at their feet, and the rest of us would slowly creep up to take the glove before they pointed their finger at you. If they did you were out.

Another taught us starboard, port, forward and aft with Akela shouting one of them and all of us having to run to the right position. It's funny looking back as you were either a cub or boy scout or not. Those that didn't wouldn't be seen dead joining such a group, but for me it was one of the best things I ever did. I think the same could be said for the rest as we all went from cubs to boy scouts till we were too old and after would remain lifelong friends.

Wintertime on the farm was just as busy as whilst most of the crops were now harvested we still had a field of sugar beet to pull and load into wagons. We didn't have a beet harvester so Dad would get some men from the village to help pull the beet, chopping off the roots and tops with a turnip knife. It was backbreaking work but one you got used to after a few days. Another job Dad would do in the winter was to clean the dykes out with a dyking spade, which was a long tapering spade specially for the purpose. There were too many dykes to do in one winter so he would only do one. Each winter we would look after a couple of horses for people. Toby and Tanner would join us at the beginning of winter and would have to be fed and exercised. They came with saddles but they were too big for me to ride on my own so I would go with Dad. Also, they liked to be together so we had to take both at the same time. Other tasks Dad would do at this time of year would be to take on some of the building projects he had planned.

I remember the first one was to build a Dutch barn out of old telegraph poles with a metal corrugated roof. Dad and a couple of other men would dig the big holes to concrete the poles in, and it was while digging one of these holes that they unearthed the skeleton of a horse. I remember them digging out a massive horse's skull and me and Paul who were there at the time being mesmerised by it. To us it looked more like some prehistoric monster's skull. The previous owners were a family called Morton who had moved from Waterside Farm to another farm at the other side of the village and still farmed with heavy horses, so we presumed this to perhaps be one of their horses which had died.

There were still periods of time for leisure, like when the snow was too deep for these kinds of jobs Dad would take us off sledging. Holme upon Spalding Moor as the name suggests is flat low-lying land but luckily with the exception of one big hill that has the church on top. So, with our big homemade sledge we would go to Church Hill in the pick-up with Jenny,

Alison and myself on the big bench seat next to Dad. The hillside was already covered with children and parents from the village with sledges of every shape and size. It was a big walk to the top but was worth it as the three of us screamed our way to the bottom. We soon learned to try and keep away from the molehills as they were rock hard. This of course wasn't easy and so we ended up in a big heap a number of times. Dad had been talking to a man that was skiing and had persuaded him to let Dad have a go on them, which he duly did deftly missing all the molehills as he slalomed his way to the bottom. He had told me once that he had been in the skiing team when he had been stationed in Germany.

He only told me once that they would ski down from Bad Harzburg to Wolfenbüttel but they were such strange names to me and I would repeat them many times over the years, usually prompted by the first fall of snow. I would remember them for the rest of my life. The sledging would come to an end when we became too cold and wet and Mum and Dad would have no trouble getting us to go to bed after such a day.

Our nana, Hannah, Dad's mother, lived in North Cave in a bungalow and sometimes Dad would take us there for the day coming back later on to pick us up. Nana was quite a thin woman who smoked quite a lot. Having said that Mum and Dad smoked quite a bit too, but Nana had perhaps been smoking for many years and had a very thin and wrinkled face. She always wore one of those coat-like button up overalls and would always wear a headscarf whenever she went out, but she always loved us going round and would keep us entertained. One day she took us into the village which had a couple of shops. She lived on the outskirts of the village so it was quite a walk, so after doing a bit of shopping and treating us to some sweets we started to make our way back. As we got to a bus stop she decided we could take the bus back up the hill just for a bit of a treat. The only time I had been on a bus was our annual school trip and I don't think Jenny or Alison had ever been on one. The bus duly arrived and we climbed aboard and found a seat, then it set off as the ticket collector came to take our fare. Nana started to look for her purse which she couldn't find in her pocket and started to look in her shopping bag. By this time we were nearly at the top of the hill so said to the ticket collector that we wanted to get off at the next stop. So, moments later we were dropped off at the top of the hill and we hadn't paid any money.

I wonder now whether she knew what she was doing all along. It certainly made our trip a little more memorable. On one of the occasions that Dad brought Nana to us for the day she had the misfortune of Grandad turning up shortly after. He only came into the veranda as he had his hobnail boots on but that was near enough for Nana. I can still remember the look that she gave me as she shook her head. I have no idea how long they had been separated at that point but she certainly wasn't on talking terms. Grandad had come to take Jenny out on Toby so wasn't going to come in the house anyway. Jenny wasn't long before she was ready to go horse riding and joined Grandad outside to make their way to the stable at the side.

Sometime later I saw Grandad walking Toby with Jenny perched on top walking down the stackyard to make their way round to the field behind the foldyard. Nana had her usual overalls on and was helping Mum with a few household chores, when all of a sudden we heard a clattering sound and heard Dad shout out. The back door was open and as I ran to see what had happened I could see Tanner running full tilt up the stackyard, and as I got into the veranda I saw Dad starting to go after him. I put my boots on and gave chase, and as I rounded the foldyard into the field Dad was about halfway across and was now walking. In the distance I could see Grandad with Toby and Jenny in one hand and Tanner in the other. As I got closer Dad had now taken hold of Tanner and Grandad had a big smile on his face. It transpired that Dad had gone to put some hay in the stables and when he opened Tanner's stable door he had bolted sending Dad flying as he sped off to find Toby. Dad had a big red mark on his arm and Grandad still smiling reached into his waistcoat pocket and gave me a Nuttall's Mintoe before we all made our way back. After that we didn't take one out without the other.

Paul Simpson had come round to see what I was doing. There were few pre-planned meetings as we rarely used our house phones preferring to just turn up on the off chance. It would be rare for one of us to be otherwise engaged, but there were times that I would have been at Malcolm's which wasn't too far across the field. We as usual had our sheaf knives on our belts and would mooch off down the stackyard without any plan on what we were going to do. As we chatted about nothing in particular we found ourselves at the tractor shed which had three bays separated by two big sturdy square wooden pillars. This was the place we would hone our knife throwing skills, so as we found ourselves there that was our first activity of the day. Standing three paces away from the pillar we would take it in turns to throw our knives to stick in the pillars. There was no target as such just an area of perforations from previous practise sessions. It was ten throws each to see who's knife stuck in the most, which over time would quite often be ten each as we would stand in the same place each time.

Coming up on a tree or random post on our travels and throwing the knife was more of a test and could end up with one of us having to jump out of the way of the knife as it bounced back from a failed throw. After we tired of throwing knives we made our way back to the sheds and into one small empty lean-to pigsty, which had a built-in trough, a small amount of straw, some empty plastic fertiliser bags and some thin poles that Dad used to mark out fields for sowing. We started with the straw. Paul had some matches in his pocket and started to put a piece of straw in his mouth and tried to light it to pretend to have a smoke, but it only burnt for a second and a nodule stopped him from sucking the smoke, so after a few failures we cut pieces of straw to lengths without a nodule in it and of varying thicknesses and then put a thinner piece inside a thicker piece and so on, four being about the maximum.

We found that we had a working cigarette of the makeshift child variety. They didn't last very long, just long enough to draw a couple of puffs of smoke into our mouths and blow it out. Once we had achieved our goal we tired of it and moved on to something else. The next task we undertook was something I think Paul had done before but I certainly hadn't. We took a couple of the poles then cut one of the plastic bags in half and using a couple of strands of Massey Harris twine tied the plastic to one end of the poles.

This we then set alight and as the plastic starts to burn drips of molten burning plastic fall from the end of the pole which make a distinctive sound. Then as we move away from each other and lift the poles higher the noise gets louder and longer and then more frequent and in a small building more dangerous as if that needed to be said. Soon the building filled with acrid smoke and the floor was covered in drips of burning plastic and finally some of the straw caught fire, at which point we both put the flaming sticks down and stamped out the straw and then used a piece of wooden board to put over the burning plastic.

We then ran out of the door coughing and spluttering which eventually turned into laughter as smoke was still flowing out of the door. The laughter soon stopped as Dad came running round the corner shouting, "What the hell are you doing?" to which I replied, "It's alright, we've put it out." Where there's smoke there's fire he said as he went through the door, and moments later he came back out to give us a good dressing down about the danger of fire. The mood was more solemn as we took to the field and made our way along the hedgerow to distance ourselves from the farm and Dad for a while. We made our way to Hodgson's shop to cheer ourselves up from the telling off we had received. We each bought a Mars bar and a large flagon of dandelion and burdock. We first ate the Mars bars and slowly drank the dandelion and burdock as we meandered our way back to the farm. Finally, we finished our drink off from the safety of our den in the hedgerow near the farm. It wasn't long before we both needed the loo of course. Because we often found ourselves some distance from the farm we were used to just peeing in the hedgerows and would have done the same now, but in this instance we had two empty bottles. So, it became a competition to see who could fill their bottle the most. This we duly did and whilst I remember the competition well I forget who won.

Holme upon Spalding Moor had an aerodrome at the other side of the village a few miles at the end of Skiff Lane, a busy aerodrome where Buccaneer jets and jet provost trainers would take off quite frequently. The sound of jets was common across the village so when Malcolm came round on his bicycle one day and the sound of jets could be heard in the distance he said we should go down to the aerodrome and have a look. Malcolm was interested in trucks and aircraft and would usually draw one or the other at school in our art lessons. He also knew the different makes of trucks and aircraft too. I liked to watch them fly over but had never thought of going to have a look and wasn't sure exactly where the aerodrome was.

However, Malcolm knew the way so off we went cycling through the village and then turning off towards the land of nod and then down Skiff Lane. After about two miles down the lane we could see a runway on the left and then further down on the right we could see the control tower, hangars and other buildings.

The road itself was a no through road and eventually led to a farm, but some way past the control tower was an area of big grassy mounds. These mounds would give us a good vantage point to hopefully see some aircraft, so we parked our bikes and climbed to the top of one of them. We sat there for a good half hour or more without seeing anything until something on one of the other mounds caught our eye and we decided to investigate. It was a bright blue piece of metal and on closer inspection turned out to be an old bonnet from a car. After looking at it for a few moments we decided to use it as a sledge. So, pulling it to the edge of the mound one of us got on and the other pushed it down the mound a little before jumping on. The first run wasn't too fast but as we paddled the grass we would go faster and faster each time. It was quite hard work so we were relieved when we saw some activity at one of the hangars.

We now sat and watched as one of the hangar doors had opened and an aircraft was being towed out by a tractor. Malcolm soon identified the aircraft as a Buccaneer which I would only have seen flying over the farm. It looked quite big on the ground as it was towed in our direction. It passed us

31

about fifty yards away at the other side of the perimeter fence and would come to rest about a hundred yards away. They had backed it up to a wooden structure at the side of the airfield. There was quite a lot of activity around it for quite some time.

A fuel tanker came over after a while and then finally we saw someone that must have been the pilot climb in. After we thought nothing was going to happen the engines started to fire up. I couldn't believe that a few hours ago I was at the farm wondering what to do and now I was sitting watching a jet aircraft start its engines. The noise just grew and grew till we had to shout at each other excitedly as we wondered what was going to happen next. We thought the aircraft would start to move towards the runway ready for take-off. The noise however just went on and on, and what we didn't realise was that they were testing the engines and the wooden structure was a muffle to soak up some of the noise. The noise at this distance was too much for us so we took to our bikes and rode off down the road till we could hear ourselves talk.

I had heard this constant noise from the farm before without knowing what was going on. We eventually made our way back but instead of going back to the farm we went round to Malcolm's house to have a drink. We would go all over the place for hours on end and would never think to take food or drink with us, and this would be what would eventually drive us home which I think Mum and Dad would know.

After a drink and perhaps a sandwich we cycled down to the factory and into a car park that backed onto the railway sidings near the station. In front of us was a wall of railway sleepers which we began to climb. Once at the top we could see there were about five compartments at the other side all made with sleepers used to store various different things, the one nearest us being full of coal. A little way beyond the compartments was the main rail line. We now began to climb around the top of the compartments holding onto the top with our feet gripping the edge of the sleepers. We had toiled away at this mindless task for about half an hour before a steam train came into the station from Market Weighton, so we stopped and took a seat on top to take a look. We had a good view from here when the train started to leave the station belching smoke and steam as it chuffed its way past us on its way to Selby. It was a sight I never tired of and would always draw my attention when they passed the farm, and this still holds true to this day.

We now had a bathroom and the toil of preparing a bath in the outhouse would become a distant memory but one we wouldn't forget. Dad would first light a fire under the copper which was like a big cauldron set into a sort of brick oven, and when this water was hot enough it was then transferred to the tin bath along with some cold water. Then us kids would take it in turns to have a bath. This was certainly nearer a weekly ritual than a daily one given the time and effort involved. So, to now have hot water in the bathroom and kitchen was a real treat.

We still used the copper from time to time to boil potato peelings for the chickens. I still remember the smell and the chickens' beaks caked with potato as we fed them. Dad would also give them handfuls of grit which I didn't fully understand at the time. It didn't look very appetising to me.

Our dog Brandy had had to have an operation on her back leg which now wouldn't heal but didn't stop her from her daily routine. She would let us know if someone was around but would never bite anyone. One car she knew as soon as it came down the drive was the vet's and she would disappear to the fields before it had reached the stackyard. She obviously associated the vet's car with the operation she'd had but how she knew from that distance was a mystery.

Mum had little time off but there were the odd nights that she would go to the pub with Dad leaving us in the hands of a babysitter which we didn't mind. I can't remember her name now but I remember her giving us something of a free rein and not being too strict so we looked forward to her coming. We would play some games but sometimes we would get a little too excited. One night I jumped up and grabbed the meat hooks on the ceiling then started to swing and brought my feet up onto two more hooks. I would be making monkey noises before I tried to bring my feet down, but the football socks that I had on got properly hooked up and I couldn't get down. I don't remember crying wolf but I couldn't get them to believe that I was stuck. My arms were aching and I was struggling to keep my grip when they realised that I wasn't kidding. Because I was quite tall and had jumped up, the babysitter couldn't reach and had to get a chair while Jenny pushed against my shoulders, and even with the chair she struggled to free both feet. Things got quite frantic before I was finally free. I certainly learned a lesson and would be in no hurry to try that again.

On nights when Mum didn't go to the pub with Dad we would sometimes play games at the table, snakes and ladders and ludo, but these would get a bit taxing for Alison being the youngest. So, we would end up playing snap which was a bit easier for her until one night when Jenny thought she had a system. Because she had been too late to say snap a number of times she took to trying to give herself a head start by saying "ssss" constantly as we put the cards down. Then one of us would say snap and Jenny was still saying "ssss", so of course we all burst out laughing. On the third time of this happening we were all laughing hysterically including Alison to the point where Alison was saying stop because she was going to wet herself, which of course made us laugh even more.

Dad in Army days

Grandma Harding, myself and Jenny

Jenny, Alison, Steven and myself, may have been looking prior to a visit of Lumley's van

Top left Steven Appleyard, Peter Holcan, Andrew Morton, Brian Holtby, Steven Pratt, Me, Richard Towse
Bottom left Mark Morton, Kevin Sherwood, Malcolm Ross, John Thornham, Steven Page.

Hardings Fireplaces workers. Far left, Grandad (Malcolm Harding), far right his brother James Harding, the young boy top centre was Mums brother John Harding

Chapter 4

Cub scouts had turned into scouts now and Akela had moved on and our scout leader was now a Mr Wilson, who worked at the St. William borstal near Market Weighton and was a likable and capable man. We enjoyed our scout evenings with a mix of discipline and games and all the same crew were there; our sixers, sort of troup leaders, were Andrew Morton and Steven Pratt. It was Andrew's parents that had owned our farm previously.

Up until now all our evenings had been spent at the wooden hut, but Mr Wilson soon had us out and about doing various things. With him working at the borstal he was able to take us to the swimming pool there. Mum and Dad had taught us to swim at an early age so I was a competent swimmer. It was a large indoor pool that we had to ourselves. I had been to a few pools in the past at Beverley and Pocklington that were all treated with chlorine, however, this one I don't think was treated with anything and certainly not chlorine. It had a light green slime on the bottom and sides but I have to say I have never been in a pool that was as clear as you could see from one end to the other and you didn't get sore eyes. It didn't get the use that some of the public pools did.

Mr Wilson was a very good swimmer and would go sub aqua diving in his spare time, so our swimming sessions weren't just recreational as we had races and lifesaving and a game of tag at the end. I remember one of the lifesaving sessions when we had first learned how to use items of clothing as buoyancy aids. You would take say a pair of jeans or a jeans top and tie a knot in the ends of the legs or arms, then holding the open end with both hands take it over your head and then bring it quickly down on the water to fill the legs or arms with air, after which you pull the open end together to keep the air in and hold with one hand. Once we had mastered this we then took it in turns to put what we had learned into practise, so someone would tread water in the deep end and wait to be saved. Then someone else wearing denim top and trousers would dive in at the shallow end and once near the person to rescue they would take either their top or trousers off, make the buoyancy aid then take them back to the shallow end. When it came to my turn I found it harder than I thought it would be, so I decided to use the top as I thought the trousers would be harder to take off. However, the top only had a few buttons near the neck so I had to pull it over my head and the wet jeans material stuck to me making it difficult. I managed but thought it might be me that would need rescuing for a few moments.

On another evening Mr Wilson took us up onto Churchill where we all practised lighting fires. There was a small wood there so he showed us some of the trees that burn well like ash because it doesn't bang and explode too much. We took any dry leaves or dead grass we could find and covered it in thin twigs and then some a little thicker. We then set it alight putting still thicker pieces on as it got going.

Once we had mastered this we built one big fire for us all to sit round and bake potatoes and toast marshmallows. When it got dark he would teach us songs, one being the "quartermaster's stores", where we would each make up and sing solo the first verse about another member of the group and then the rest would join in and sing the chorus. So, Malcolm may have sung:

"There was Dave, Dave, being very brave,
 in the stores, in the stores
 There was Dave, Dave, being very brave,
 in the quartermaster's stores."

Then we would all sing:

"My eyes are dim. I cannot see,
 I have not brought my specs with me.
 I have not brought my specs with me."

And then the next member would start the next verse and so on. Of course, you were limited to what would rhyme with

39

different people's names, but some had nicknames which helped and being eight year olds it caused a giggle or two and brought characters to the fore. He then finished the evening by telling us a true story about when he was a boy scout camping in the glens of Scotland.

He was in a group of six who were out orienteering using a map and compass to find their way around the glen when a thick fog fell and they got lost. They spent hours wandering around before they came across a bothey, a cottage used by shepherds or hikers for shelter, which was empty. They felt relieved to find shelter and made themselves at home as best they could, and when night fell they retired to the one upstairs bedroom to bed down with what little bedding they could find. Then, just before they fell asleep, they heard the front door open and close and then footsteps at the bottom of the stairs. One of them shouted, "Hello, who is it?" to no answer. They were now all standing and wondering who this could be when the footsteps could be heard slowly climbing the stairs. Again, they shouted, "Who is it?" again to no answer. One of them had a small torch which they now shone at the door, the sound of the footsteps getting louder and louder as did their cries.

Finally, they saw a loft hatch above and one by one began to scramble into the darkness of the loft until just one was left. The door handle was now turning as the boys started to pull the last one up. Then, just as they thought they had him safe, someone grabbed his leg and then started to pull it, just as I am now pulling your leg. At that point our two sixers Mark and Steven who had secretly been primed by Mr Wilson to slowly leave the fireside near the end of the story now burst from two sides shouting "AHHH!" at the top of their voices frightening the rest of us to death.

One job I did before I went to school was to fetch the milk from the end of the lane. We had a milk crate under a tree near the main road and if you didn't pick it up early the blue tits would start to help themselves to the cream through the foil top. The milkman would come very early so even with me picking it up first thing the early bird had sometimes already got the cream. In the wintertime the frost had sometimes frozen the cream at the top lifting the foil off the bottle by half an inch or so before I had picked it up. I was going to school on my bike now or would walk if I had a puncture. Alison had started the infant class so Mum was still taking Jenny and Alison in the car. The Ford Popular had gone and we now had a Hillman Imp. I can remember Dad being taken up with the engine being at the back. It wasn't in any way new but it started better than the Popular did and wouldn't have any great mileage to do either.

The school had an open fronted, tile pitched roofed bike shed which had dozens of bats hanging from the rafters, something we took for granted then but wouldn't know where to go to see one now.

Another good friend of mine at school was Stephen Atkinson, or "Fatty Acko" as he was called being the only fat boy in the school. Kids can of course be cruel and fun could be poked at almost anyone. My name was Barker so kids would shout "Woof, woof" or say "If you want to buy a dog buy a barker." You learned not to bite if I dare say that and they would gradually tire of it, but I would be lying if I said it didn't bother me, especially when you had about ten kids shouting it. Stephen was a funny and entertaining lad and was fun to be around. I don't remember him coming to the farm as I would usually go round to his house after school as he lived nearby. He had a small fish tank which he would put some frog spawn in, then we would go to a nearby pit and catch a couple of newts and put them in. Then behind his house there was a small pond that had a lot of sticklebacks in, so using a small amount of line with a small hook on and a piece of chopped worm we would catch a couple, then using an empty jar take them to the fish tank. Over the following weeks I would go round to see the tadpoles slowly turn to small frogs before he finally released them back to the pond.

At school Mr Asker would amongst other things teach us English giving spelling tests or getting us to write short stories. I remember one that I did which started, "The big black bird blotted the sky". I don't remember any more of it and I only remember that because my mother read it one day, and if we were out and about and we saw a crow she would say the big black bird blotted the sky, which my sisters would then start to say and later still my brothers would do the same. So it was forever embedded in the Barker psyche.

Near the end of the lesson Mr Asker would read to us, and one book I remember well was *Worzel Gummidge*. We would sit there in complete silence spellbound by the story and the delivery and couldn't wait for the next lesson. The cycle ride home from school was usually uneventful, chatting to friends as they rode home or riding slowly chatting to friends as they walked home. Then as I reached the end of the village I would usually be on my own for the last half mile or more of open road, till one day I noticed a big bird in the distance sat on the street light. Then as I got closer it took off and started to fly towards me. I could now see that it was a large blue and green parrot. Wow! I thought, a parrot. I remember wishing some of my friends were still with me to share the moment. Who was going to believe that I had seen a parrot? That thought soon left as the parrot now started to dive bomb me giving out a loud squawk as it whizzed past my ear as I ducked. I was now pedalling for my life as the parrot now turned and started another attack from behind, again screeching out as I felt the draft from its wings. This relentless dive bombing went on until I reached the safety of the willow trees. Instead of just walking into the house and telling Mum I had seen a parrot on my way home from school like I first imagined, I was now running in breathless and hardly able to get the words out.

It transpired the parrot belonged to Baldry's who had a market garden and coach business a couple of miles further out of the village. Sheila Baldry was in my class at school so I soon learned that it was her pet parrot that had escaped. It was some days before the parrot was enticed back to its cage and so I had to run the gauntlet of the parrot till then. The parrot would return in the months that followed from time to time as it learned its new routine.

Grandma and Grandad (Harding) that lived opposite were moving. My grandmother didn't like the regular sound of the jet aircraft so were going back to the relative quiet of South Cave. We would still see them of course, just not as often.

In their place had moved the Macphearson family. Mr and Mrs Macphearson had two children, Andrew and Ann. Andrew was a year older than me and would start to go to our school and over the coming months we got to know each other as we would end up travelling the last stint home from school together. Another nice lad that would in time join the scout group.

We had similar interests like fishing, swimming and exploring. Andrew, having a mop of ginger hair, stood out in the crowd and took some time to be accepted by some of the other kids at school. It didn't take him long to explore the open land at the back of their house. Being at the other side of the main road to us, it was an area neither I or Paul had ventured having plenty to contend with such as the foulness, the railway and the farm. So, getting to know Andrew over the coming months opened up a whole new playground. There was a woodland across the field that had a five feet high carpet of ferns from one side to the other, within which we opened a network of tunnels making the biggest den I had ever seen.

One Friday on our way home from school Andrew asked if I fancied going swimming the following day as he had found a pond further across the fields that could be our own private swimming pool, and as we had hot weather at the time I agreed. So, late morning the next day with towel in hand we headed off across the fields to what looked like a lot of bushes. I was expecting to see a clear inviting body of water with the sun glinting off it, instead we were now fighting our way through hawthorn bushes having left our clothes and shoes in the field. We reached the other side of the bushes and were now standing in a foot of water with thick black sludge underfoot with dead twigs and small branches all around.

The whole circumference of the pond was the same with no open bankside and was about fifty yards across. I was of course having second thoughts when Andrew took a few more strides and lunged forward into the unknown and began to swim breaststroke to the sound of heavy breathing. I was duty bound to follow so off I went following in Andrew's wake as we made our way to the other side. As we neared the other side we could feel bits of branch then our hands would go into the black mud as we scrambled to stand up, still huffing and puffing from the cold and adrenaline. The bushes looked even thicker here so there was only one thing for it, we would have to swim back. So, turning round in the thick mud we made our way back to the silent centre of the pond with our heavy breathing for company. When we got to the other side we trudged our way back through the bushes and into the field, our feet and hands covered in black sludge and scratches on our arms from the hawthorn.

Well that was one wild swimming venue I wouldn't be going to again I said as we made our way back across the field with clothes and shoes in hand. Andrew agreed but I got the feeling he would quite happily have gone again at the drop of a hat.

Dad had three lads that would come to help periodically, Gordon Fox and two brothers called Garth and Lance. They were at college and later university so would come in their holidays or weekends to earn themselves a bit of extra cash. They were good with us kids and would joke around with us when they came in for lunch or sometimes breakfast. Gordon lived in the village so would walk to the farm, but Lance and Garth lived in another village so Dad bought a Vespa scooter for them to come to work on. They always caused a stir when they arrived at the farm, and if we heard the scooter coming down the lane we would run to greet them. The lane to the farm was fairly rough so they looked quite comical as they bounced and wove their way round the potholes, exaggerating slightly when they saw us watching.

It had come round to potato picking time again and the three lads had come to help out. Dad had been up early and had already spun out a couple of rows of potatoes with the potato spinner which was fastened to the back of the tractor. It had a big blade which went under the row lifting it up a bit and into the path of spinning tines, which threw the whole row sideways spreading it out over four or five feet leaving all the potatoes on the surface. We were picking and putting the potatoes straight into four stone paper bags, so the potatoes needed to be dry which is why Dad had spun some out early. He had also put the baskets out ready and placed packs of paper bags across the field in preparation.

So, after a period of idle chat we began to pick, Gordon and Lance on one row and Dad and Garth on the other. I would alternate to keep us all together as we made our way across the field, and when the baskets were full one would hold a bag open while the other emptied the baskets. Halfway across the field Dad would break off to go and spin out another couple of rows further across the field to make sure we always had some drying out. It was important not to spin too many out especially if there was a chance of a shower. Also, towards the end of the day we only wanted enough so we had finished picking at three o'clock giving time to gather up and weigh the bags we had picked. So, while we picked the last few potatoes of the day Dad would trundle off and take the spinner off and put a low trailer on. Then he would sometimes let me drive the tractor and trailer along as they loaded the open bags on the back.

We would then take the trailer to the barn where they were going to be stored and set up the scales. Each bag was then weighed and tied. The top of the bag was gathered together as tight as possible and then a metal wire with loops either end was wrapped around, then a twizzler, a long-handled tool with a hook at the end, was put through the hoops. When you pulled the twizzler it twisted the wire round sealing the bag ready for storage. This job would go on over the next few weeks along with all the other daily tasks of feeding pigs and putting new bedding down, exercising the horses and more, so days at this time of year for Dad were long and hard but I know he enjoyed every minute.

Another job I would help with after the potatoes was to pull and store the carrots. The land round Holme upon Spalding Moor was sandy land so much so that on windy days the sand would blow off open fields and create drifts across the lanes and roads, sometimes six inches or more deep. This sandy land was however good for growing carrots so in the early years the carrots would be pulled and put into a tipper trailer by hand. We would pull the carrots and lay them in rows close to each other, then chop the tops off with a sharp spade and using a sippit, a multi tined fork, scoop them up and into the trailer. When the trailer was full we would take it to the side of the field and tip them out into a heap. Subsequent loads were tipped at the same side to create a long heap of carrots. After each day of harvesting Dad would shovel soil from round the heap onto the carrots covering them with about five inches of soil on the sides leaving a few feet of the top exposed. This would then be covered in straw. This was called a pie and would keep the carrots into the winter when a better price could be achieved.

The first couple of years Dad didn't take any kind of holiday but working every day no matter how much you enjoy it can take its toll. Finally, Mum and Dad decided now was the time as they had the opportunity to borrow a VW campervan, and Gordon, Lance and Garth were happy and capable to take care of the animals while we were away. Mum was pregnant again now so that could also have been a factor.

The van was loaded up with all the supplies necessary to keep three kids and a baby happy for a week. Brandy was staying at the farm to be looked after by the lads. No campsites had been booked, indeed no firm destination had been planned, just to head north perhaps to the Scottish Borders. Jenny and myself took it in turns to sit up front with Dad while Mum kept an eye on Alison and Steven in the back. We headed north stopping periodically to try out the stove to make tea and have something to eat, then towards the end of the day Dad would look for a suitable lay-by to park up for the night. It was all exciting stuff as Dad pushed up the roof to reveal our bed for the night, and the smell of burning gas was new to us and would become a big part of the camping experience, not just because food was on the way but was unique to camping and will always remind me of those times.

Sleeping was a cosy arrangement with Jenny and Alison at one end and me at the other, while Steven slept with Mum and Dad. It was always an early start as Dad would be itching to get breakfast on the go which was always bacon and eggs and would be eaten outside if the weather allowed. We finally reached the Scottish Borders and for Dad it was all about the countryside seclusion and a river, and back then that was something that was easy to achieve. So, we would find ourselves on the grass verge of a country road next to a stream, something we kids didn't seem to tire of. The novelty of the campervan was still strong. Dad was certainly in his element with a rod and reel and small amount of gear that he had brought along, and he would head off up the stream to fish for trout.

Every other day we would move on to pastures new, especially if no fish were to be had. We always knew when he had caught one as we would see the smile on his face before we saw the fish as he made his way back. The fish were never very big but he would always cook and eat them, Mum too, but it wasn't something that appealed to the rest of us. Always being on the move kept us happy wondering what was round the next bend. From the Scottish Borders we made our way across and down into the Lake District having our fair share of rain. Sitting in the van having our dinner in the pouring rain was something we all enjoyed, a feeling which may have changed had it rained every day. The weather was good though as we made camp north of Ambleside, and again we had found an empty lay-by with a big wide shallow river meandering into the field opposite.

In the morning after breakfast we all headed out across the field to a big sweeping bend in the river which had created a large shallow shingle beach. It was here that Dad showed us the magic of skimming stones, picking out a round flat stone and throwing it low across the water to skip along ten or twelve times. It was indeed magic. We spent some considerable time perfecting the art to varying degrees of success, remembering well the moment your stone skipped across the water. Here too it was ideal for us all to take a paddle in our own little piece of heaven. The same place now is a different story, a large pay and display car park and a stone wall in place of the beach frequented by hundreds of people. A sign of the times no doubt, but I feel privileged and fortunate to have experienced those times.

There were a few times that I would walk along the side of the railway tracks but not on my own. We crossed the railway lines many times on our own adhering to the metal signs saying Stop, Look and Listen. Trains were fairly infrequent but we still took care when crossing. However, there were times when I would go down the side of the tracks with Grandad. There were two sets of tracks and we would walk down one side and come back on the other. We would have a potato basket each and walk along picking up coal, and it was surprising how much coal would fall from the trains. We could get two basketfuls from about half a mile of track. It would be my grandad's something for nothing policy or waste not want not I suppose. We would only go a few times in the autumn and winter and I don't ever remember a train coming, so whether Grandad knew the train times I don't know. The only heating the farm had was the coal fire in the living room. There was a fireplace in one of the bedrooms but I don't ever remember it being lit. The other time we would venture down the side of the tracks was to go bramble picking. There was an abundance of really nice brambles that no one else would pick so it didn't take long to pick a couple of bowlfuls. Grandad had a walking stick to pull down the bramble laden bows that we couldn't reach. I don't ever remember him using a walking stick so he must have brought it along especially for the occasion. Mum would then make bramble or bramble and apple pie. She would regularly bake and my favourites were lemon, custard and curd tarts.

A couple of photos of Grandad near his house with a couple of working horses

Campervan stop on our way to Scotland

The skimming stones beach in the lake district

Hannah Barker (Nana) in her overalls

Paul had come round again. He had his Wellingtons on and had a fishing net in his hand and suggested we go down to the foulness to see what we could catch, so I put my Wellingtons on and rooted out a glass jar and off we went to the river. The first stop was nearly always the bridge to have a look at the resident menacing pike underneath. From here too we could see numerous small roach and further downriver the bigger roach could be seen breaking the surface. We then walked downriver to where it runs alongside the railway lines; the corner here is deep and has a big concrete drain running into it. The river from here now gets wider and shallow as it follows the railway. It was at this point that we got in the water and with one of us moving stones while the other held the net downriver made our way along to see what we could catch. Soon we had a fish in the net and went to the bank side to put it in the jar of water to have a better look. It was a bullhead or miller's thumb as it is sometimes called, not the prettiest of fish but an interesting fish to see close up. We kept working our way along until we had quite a few in the jar. All were the same size and we didn't catch anything different so we put them back. The river now turns and goes under the railway and as we walk under the brick arch our voices and footsteps echo. Under here the stones were a lot bigger and the water a bit deeper, nearly to our boot tops, so was a bit more precarious as we moved the bigger stones.

Suddenly a big eel slipped past our net and went under another stone almost making us fall over with surprise. We now made sure the net was pressed a little into the gravel and this time we had the eel in the net, then, holding the top of the net just above the water, we watched the eel swim around the net so we could check him out. Then we slowly dipped the net in to let him escape and watched him swim off to another hiding place. As we were still standing in the middle of the river congratulating ourselves on our catch, a bottle came bobbing down the river between us and I picked it up for no reason other than it was right in front of me. As I did Paul said jokingly, "Message in a bottle," and as I looked closer there was indeed a piece of paper in it. Paul couldn't believe it when I said, so we made our way out of the river to have a closer look. We took the top off and pulled out the piece of paper which was indeed a message. It was from a farm about three miles away. The source of the river itself is only about six miles away so we knew it couldn't have come far. It had today's date on and must have only been put in that morning. There was a phone number to ring, so we made our way back to the farm to show Mum. Mum later rang the people to tell them of our find, and they were of course surprised that it had been picked up so soon but asked if we could put it back again to hopefully be found further afield. It was the next day when I put it back in the river for it to continue on its way.

We were at home when Mum gave birth to Richard. I remember hearing his first cry from the bedroom above. Mum had two babies to contend with now, so we would help out where we could if it only meant behaving ourselves. I remember Brandy doing her bit to help out. One day Dad came in to get Brandy to go with him. She was sat at the bottom of the stairs and no matter how much Dad coerced her she wouldn't move. It turned out Mum was in the kitchen and had left Richard upstairs asleep in his cot. It appeared she was keeping guard and didn't move until Mum later brought him down.

It was scout night the evening after Richard was born so I had news to tell the boys. It was Andrew's first night as a scout too so he joined me as we made our way across the village on foot to the scout hut. It was a tough first night for Andrew as we had an evening of learning semaphore, a way of signalling with flags, which I had done before and found difficult. We also had a small ceremony that was held to award badges to different members for activities they had achieved. It was quite regimental standing to attention and saluting each other, but towards the end we played some of the usual games to liven things up a bit. Andrew said that he had enjoyed the evening as we headed back. It was dark now but there were plenty of streetlights to light our way. We travelled through the village and had just begun to head out into the countryside when we could see someone walking towards us. We kept walking until the figure came to the next streetlight. This person had a hat with a brim on, a long raincoat and Wellington boots which we could see shining slightly from the light. He also had both arms up near his left ear. Oh my god, it's Charlie. I had seen him in the village a few times, a mysterious character who walked along with a limp, always dressed the same and always carried a radio to his ear, and here he was heading in our direction in the dark. Well it was too scary for us so we beat a hasty retreat running back to Hodgson's corner shop and then down Station Road to the milk factory and the train station, looking back all the while and didn't stop till we reached the station. We then caught our breath before we went down the side of the railway in the pitch dark to Holly Lane, something we found a lot less scary than facing Charlie. As we slowly made our way up Holly Lane which led back to the main road we started to see the streetlights. All was clear but we still moved slowly and quietly till we got to the farm lane. Then we bid each other goodnight and both of us ran home like the wind not even daring to look round.

Malcolm's parents were quite religious and would attend church every Sunday. Religion played a big part of our junior school days, having the daily assembly singing hymns and celebrating all the religious events as they came along. So, when Malcolm asked if I wanted to go with him bell ringing I said yes. It wasn't something that I had ever thought of trying but it sounded quite exciting. So, one evening after school, I went with him to bell ringing practise. Mr Hazler was the vicar of the village, a short and rounded man who always wore a trilby and smoked a pipe when out and about in the village. He was a nice man who always had time for a chat but didn't have anything to do with the bell ringing, so the evening consisted of four adults from the village and six or seven kids, most of who were older than Malcolm and myself. They seemed keen to get new blood interested in the church and giving them lessons at bell ringing was probably a good place to start. It was a lot more complicated than I had first thought and quite nerve-racking, especially when they explained if you didn't slow it down at the top as the rope went up it could break the stay. I was quite tall for my age but Malcolm had to stand on a small stool, so after showing us how to ring the bell and explain exactly what was happening we each had a go. We stood with someone hovering over us to make sure we didn't let go or miss the catch, and we then after putting one hand through a loop in the end of the rope pulled the rope down bringing the bell off the stay. The sally, the woollen handle, would come down past you almost to the floor, then as it comes up you have to catch it, let it go up a bit, then pull it down again, this time letting it go past you as it goes up keeping a bit of pressure on the rope to let the bell rest on the stay again. This was just one ring and if you were going to carry on ringing you would just stop it from hitting the stay at the top and do the same procedure again. We kept up the practise for quite a few weeks until it got serious. Once they started to get us to ring in sequence to create a proper bell ringing peal so that you were to ring third and then seventh and so on. It became more complicated than we had bargained for and we dropped out, preferring instead to play games with Keith and Michael.

Mr Wilson had booked us in for our first scout camp which was going to be for a week at a place called Givendale and had given us a list of things that we needed. The only camping that I had done, if you could call it that, was sleeping in a tent in Paul's garden a few years previously, which didn't end well. The tents back then didn't have zips but had three or four sets of cord or ribbon that you tied up with a bow. During the night I woke up not realising where I was in the pitch dark, found the doorway but couldn't undo the ties. I ended up breaking my way out sitting on the dewy grass wanting Mum and Dad. But things were different now and Mum had got me the gear that we needed: a rucksack, not the sort that you would climb Everest with, just a dumpy rucksack with a big pocket either side. Then I had a set of billy cans, three oblong pans with folding handles that fit inside each other, knife, fork and spoon that clipped together, and an enamel mug, plate and bowl. On the last scout meeting before the camp Mr Wilson had shown us how to pack our rucksacks, first putting clothing in the bottom that you wouldn't need for a few days, with other things nearer the top that you would need sooner. The things like knife, fork, spoon, matches, torch, toothbrush, soap, etc, went in the side pockets with billy cans tied at the side and sleeping bag on top. He gave us all a checklist of everything that we would need, including types and quantities of clothing.

So, the big day had arrived. We had our bags packed and Dad had taken me in the pick-up to the scout hut. One by one everyone arrived dressed in their scout uniforms with packed rucksacks by their sides. Expectant banter filled the air as our mode of transport arrived. It was an open backed army wagon with a canvas covered frame on the back. Packed at the front were our tents, spades, hammers, food and everything else we would need. We all clambered in packing the rucksacks down the centre as we all sat down the sides. Finally, we were off waving goodbye to our respective parents as we set off down the road. None of us had been to Givendale before and had no idea how far away it was. As it turned out we didn't have to sit too long in the back of the drafty truck, for after just over half an hour we were turning off down an old farm road. We now travelled about a mile down the rough farm track being jostled around in the back, which we all found quite amusing before we finally came to a stop. We all climbed out to find ourselves at the bottom of a large wide dale with mature woodland growing up the sides, then further down the woodland gave way to open grass dale sides. To one side was a raised plateau of grass with a big wooden hut upon it with a flagpole flying the scouts' *fleur-de-lys*. There was no time for exploring as Mr Wilson began to direct operations, and he had another scout leader with him to help out. We began by choosing a place for our respective tents. There were twelve of us with four to a tent, so we split up into three groups to erect them. The tents were quite big but simple, just a pole either end held up with a few guy ropes and sides you just pulled out and pegged. Then after we rolled out a ground sheet our bags were placed inside.

The next job we had to do under guidance from Mr Wilson was to put up a latrine, which meant finding a suitable area some distance from the main camp, digging a hole and putting a collapsible seat over it, then putting a simple canvas structure round it. Once the camp was all set Mr Wilson showed us all round the site. There was a small brook that ran through the whole site and off to one side next to the scout hut from a little copse of trees was a spring of fresh water that came out of the ground and ran into the brook further down. This would be our supply of water for the week which was quite handy. Our next task was to scour the woodland to collect a supply of wood remembering what we had been taught. Each tent would have their own fire for cooking, but we wouldn't be lighting the fires and cooking until teatime so had sandwiches and soft drinks as we still had our beds to make and gear to sort out. We also made tripods to hold a pot above the fire. The weather was nice and warm and it really was a super site.

Later in the afternoon Mr Wilson showed us two concrete walls a little further down the dale. We puzzled as to what they were for. They ran parallel to each other about twelve feet apart, sixty feet long and about three and a half feet high. It wasn't until Mr Wilson got us to sweep all the sheep droppings and soil off the concrete floor and put some wooden boards in the ends that we guessed that it might be a swimming pool. He then showed us a gully which led downhill from the brook to the top corner of the pool.

After redirecting part of the brook with some pieces of wood the water started to run along the gully into the pool. This we watched for a time and would be left overnight to fill up checking periodically for leaks. We certainly weren't expecting to have our own swimming pool and couldn't wait for tomorrow. We then went to have a look at the hut which was just an oblong wooden hut with a wooden floor where he said we would gather at evening time. He said sometimes Givendale would host a district camp where other scout groups would come from Market Weighton and Pocklington, but this week we had the place to ourselves. It was now time to start our evening meal which was going to be a stew, nothing too complicated for our meagre cooking skills and facilities. So, while two from each tent would start the fire the other two would prepare the vegetables and cut the meat, and the water container would be filled from the spring ready to put in the cooking pot. Mr Wilson kept the food in the truck and would allocate rations to each group. Once the fire had died back we set the tripod up to hang the pot of stew on then took it in turns to keep an eye on it giving the occasional stir. This was all new to most of us so it was all done under the watchful eye of our scout leaders. Eventually, when the stew was deemed to be cooked, we filled our billy cans and with a handful of bread sat round the fire to enjoy our labours.

After we had eaten and washed the pots we had time to explore before we all met up in the scout hut for our end of day celebration. Mr Wilson gave a talk on our achievements of the day and spoke of some of the plans he had lined up for the rest of the week. We then finished off the evening with a rousing song or two. After we had brushed our teeth and settled into our sleeping bags and the excitement of the day ebbed away, we were left with the silence of the sheltered dale, punctuated by the periodical "baa" from distant sheep that we hadn't noticed during the day but had now made their presence known. Nobody wanted to oversleep in the morning as there was too much excitement and anticipation for the day ahead, so fires were soon lit and frying pans with bacon and eggs were soon sizzling. After breakfast was finished, pots put away and tents tidy, we all made our way to the swimming pool which was now brimming over with fresh brook water. We wouldn't be swimming just yet but the woods were taken out to stop the flow of water. Mr Wilson now had a task to perform for which he needed our help. He had already picked out a suitable tree and placed a pile of ropes, pulleys and straps at its base. After explaining what he was going to do he began to climb the tree with a rope hooked over his shoulder and cable and couplings hanging from his belt. A couple of us held the rope free of the branches as he climbed about three quarters of the way up the tree. This was a big beech tree so he was a long way up as he fastened the rope to the main trunk of the tree. The rest of the rope was then unfurled some eighty or ninety yards which took a few of us to do as it was quite a thick rope. This was attached to a big metal peg that was hammered into the ground before Mr Wilson climbed the tree again carrying a harness. Then after attaching the harness he came flying out from the branches zipping down the rope before coming to a skidding halt at the bottom. We were all looking at each other with nervous excitement as we had all climbed trees before but had never done anything like this.

Mr Wilson now stood before us with a big beaming smile saying, "Right, who wants to be first?" Whilst we all wanted to have a go no one wanted to be first. Eventually, our sixer Andrew stepped forward. There were a few teething problems to sort out and a couple of pegs had to be put in at the base of the tree to help climb the first ten feet. Then a light rope was fastened from above to pull the harness up before Andrew was ready to make his run. Mr Wilson was at the top to make sure we were fastened properly and our other scout leader was at the bottom to help steady our fall. After Andrew made his run everybody wanted to be next, but after forming an orderly queue we each had a go. I had climbed trees many times before so had no problem but this was high, and even with Mr Wilson helping with the harness this was a scary and precarious affair. A loop of rope went over your shoulders and under your arms, then you put your hands through two hoops at the end of a metal bar with grips on. You then held on to the grips and off you went. It was certainly scary for the first few runs but we soon became old hands.

After a mid-afternoon break to have something to eat and let the adrenaline levels drop we were already thinking of the swimming pool, but we had more wood to collect and other chores and things to do before then. It would be almost five o'clock before we were able and ready to take a swim. Once we had the okay to go swimming it was a race to be first in. One side of the wall was built up against the dale side so this was our point of entry running down the grass bank and jumping in as soon as we got there, and even with the pool standing in the hot sun all day the water was freezing and our first swim didn't last too long. Over the coming days we became proficient at lighting fires and cooking. We would fly from the tree with confidence and the swimming pool got warmer. We learned to identify more trees and would put some knots we had learned to the test. The remaining days flew by and it didn't seem like a week had passed before we were rumbling along in the back of the truck once again, with much to tell when we returned home.

Dad was building a Nissen hut and had a wagon load of breeze blocks, sand and cement delivered. Even with the help of the lads it was quite a large undertaking. Footings had to be dug and long breeze block walls four course high would be built for the sides. An arched roof of asbestos would be put on before the ends were blocked in with doors and windows in place. The building when finished was going to house more pigs freeing up room in the other barn for some calves Dad had designs on buying. Work on the building was in full swing with Gordon, Lance and Garth in attendance. Grandad had turned up on his bike and he was going to scythe down nettles and long grass in the orchard and other areas of the farm which were overgrown. He would scythe roadsides for the council especially in front of signs and places of poor visibility. I liked to watch him as he set himself sweeping the scythe round and shuffling along with each sweep, then periodically stopping to sharpen the scythe. He would stand it on its handle, then holding the thick end of the blade take a long sharpening stone out of his pocket. This he would then sweep down one side of the blade to the end and then back to the top to sweep down the other side. This he repeated in a fast-flowing motion before setting off again. He would sometimes let me have a go but he made it look easy which it certainly wasn't.

At lunchtime we would all gather together for sandwiches and tea, then as Dad would smoke a cigarette Grandad would tell stories to the lads. One I remember was when he was cleaning out a dyke on the side of the road. He said he was in the bottom of a dyke near to a gateway to a field with a big hedge in front of him, when a car pulled over near to the gateway and a chap climbed out. He said this chap hadn't seen him in the bottom of the dyke and passed through the gateway round the back of the hedge to end up the other side opposite Grandad. He then with his back to the hedge proceeded to pull his trousers down to relieve himself. For a second Grandad was bemoaning his luck when he had an idea. He said he popped his long spade under the hedge to catch the unmentionable then swiftly bringing it back to empty to one side. Then he watched as the chap pulled and fastened his trousers before turning round to check out his efforts before moving on. As nothing was to be seen he could see a slight panic had gripped the man, as he now spun around again to double check before again pulling his trousers down to see if things had been caught inadvertently. Of course, everyone laughed at the story not knowing if the man finally saw Grandad or if it were indeed true.

Summer holidays I will always remember as being long and hot and the best time ever, and I don't think rose tinted glasses had anything to do with it. They couldn't have been invented then, certainly as far as the temperature was concerned. I have so many memories of water fights and swimming in ponds and rivers and It wasn't as if I were a hardy soul. The month of June was a time I always got a suntan, not from sunbathing of course but from hoeing sugar beet. We had our own beet but Dad would also hoe some beet for other people. One field I remember well was on the outskirts of a village near York where both Dad and I found a Roman coin each, which I would proudly show everyone including Mr Asker our schoolteacher. However, back to the summer holidays. They seemed so long that I remember almost forgetting some people at school when we eventually returned.

So many days would start at the bridge down at the foulness; locally we would pronounce it the "fooner". Paul and I had decided to have a go at catching the big scary pike under the bridge. Paul had brought his fishing rod and reel and we had dug a few big worms at the farm. We now marched down the track armed and ready, our sole purpose to catch the big scary pike under the bridge. It was Paul's rod so he was going to catch the fish, something I was more than happy to let him do. As we neared the bridge part of me hoped it wouldn't be there, but there it was large as life in its usual place resting stationary near the bottom with just the movement of its fins to hold its position. Our plan which hadn't been given a lot of thought was to put the worm on the hook and slowly lower the hook into the water from the bridge directly above the fish.

So, with great expectation and fear of the unknown Paul began to lower away. The worm landed on the water and began to sink slowly to the bottom. The moment is so imprinted in my memory for whatever reason that I remember the worm landing roughly ten inches in front of the pike and five inches to the left. I think it was this fact that helped cement the moment, because to start with the pike didn't do anything and Paul was going to move the worm, but just before he did the pike's fins sped up a little and started to move forward ever so slowly, which got both of our heart rates up and both of us saying, "It's moving! It's moving!" It moved forward about five inches and for a second we thought it was going to swim off, but then it started to turn and move closer and closer to the worm. We were now beside ourselves as the pike stopped with the worm just to the left of its mouth. Then all of a sudden it moved its head sideways and scooped the worm up. With the worm in its mouth and our hearts in ours we prepared for our next move. We looked at each other with nervous grins before Paul tightened slowly on the reel, then with what seemed like an explosion the pike tore off upriver at breakneck speed almost pulling the rod out of Paul's hands. Then just as fast as the rod had bent double all went slack. Our expectation and surge of adrenaline turned to disbelief and disappointment as we stood on our tiptoes with just the sound of our hearts in our ears before we relaxed and Paul wound the line in to find it had broken.

What we learned later was that we should have had a metal trace at the bottom and fastened the hook onto that. The pike's teeth had simply cut the line. That might have been the end of the fishing trip as we had failed in the task we had set, but Paul wanted to fish on and said we should try further up the river. I agreed but I hadn't got my rod and gear so I said I would run back and pick it up and catch up with him. Paul had walked quite some way upriver as it meandered across the fields, and it wasn't too long before I had picked up my rod and dug a few more worms and was heading off across the fields to join him.

There was a little bridge upriver made of railway sleepers which was about as far as I had been previously. I had caught some nice minnows here before but Paul was in new territory further on. He was on a sandy beach with the river flowing round him so I decided to fish the deep-looking corner before him. The river had scoured out the bankside and I was fishing from the top of the bank about eight feet above the water. I set my rod up, put on a worm and cast it in. After putting the rod on a rod rest I had a wander along to see Paul, and it goes without saying that we were still very much in the trial and error stage of fishing. We weren't sure what we might catch but we were happy with our endeavours.

After about twenty minutes I decided to go back to my rod, only when I got there it had gone. My rod rest was still there but no rod. I quickly ran back to tell Paul and he came to investigate but there was no sign of it. Paul thought it might have fallen in. I couldn't see how but whatever had happened it was the end of my fishing trip and would be for Paul too as he hadn't had any bites.

The very next day when Paul came round, we decided to try and solve the mystery of the missing rod. We thought if we could drag something across the river we might snag it if it was there. We took one of Dad's hoes which we knew wasn't long enough so we tied on one of his marker poles to the end. Then with this contraption over Paul's shoulder we marched off across the field to see what we could do. As we walked along the top of the riverbank and neared the corner where I had fished I saw an eel swimming away from the deep bend in a shallow section of the river. I pointed it out to Paul who then looked and noticed a float about four feet behind it. Then we realised the eel wasn't going anywhere. So that was the answer to our mystery, the eel had pulled my rod in. It didn't take us long to snag the line and pull the eel in but it did take a while to unhook the it, Paul finally getting the hook out as I wrestled with the eel to keep it still. Once we had returned the eel we started to pull on the line and thankfully the rod and reel emerged no worse for wear. The experience of unhooking the eel put us off catching eels with rod and line and still makes me sigh when I catch one to this day.

My days playing round at Malcolm's house was something I always enjoyed. In the earlier years we would play with Scalextric if we were allowed as it took up quite a bit of space, but more often than not it would be with our collection of Dinky and Corgi cars. We would hound our parents to buy us cars that would be advertised after certain TV series brought them to our attention. One of the first was the white Volvo seen on the TV series *The Saint* starring Roger Moore. We would seldom miss an episode and just had to have the car when they arrived in the shops. We liked the Volvo which didn't have any moving parts or opening doors, but it had what looked like diamonds for headlights that twinkled as light would hit them which made the car very appealing. The next was the car from the series *The Man from Uncle*. It was not the prettiest of cars but it had a button on top which when pressed an arm holding a gun would pop in and out of the side windows, which again made it a must have. Another must have was the James Bond Aston Martin with machine guns popping out at the front, bulletproof shield coming up at the back and the ejector seat throwing a man out of the roof. There weren't many of my friends that didn't have this one. Another popular car was the Batmobile. I can still remember taking it out of the box for the first time and being struck by the immaculate shiny black paintwork and spending ages just looking at it. It seemed too good to play with but play with it we did with none of them ever seeing their boxes again. The Ross household was my second home at times as I would often eat there and sleep over the odd night. I was always made to feel welcome and joined them on nights out. I remember going with them to see a Christmas pantomime and also to the pictures to see the Bond film *On Her Majesty's Secret Service*, a good film to see with your friends at the big screen. My dad wasn't a big cinema fan but Mum took us to see *Ring of Bright Water* and *The Railway Children* some years later which we all enjoyed. As we got older the Dinky and Corgi toys were resigned to the cupboard and we would spend our time playing board games especially if the weather was inclement. To begin with we would play games like ludo and would play each other at draughts, but then for quite a while we progressed to Monopoly which can be quite a long drawn-out game and would usually end when Mrs Ross would tell us it was time we went out for some fresh air. The last games I remember us playing were Risk and the other was a game called Campaign, and once we had played these Monopoly was confined to the cupboard too. Risk was a good game where you acquired armies and tried to take over the world and it didn't take too long to play, which meant we would usually play to a finish. But Campaign we really liked. It was a clever game in which you each controlled armies, however there was a lot of strategy involved similar to a game of chess which would hold our interest for hours.

One of the great things about being a child in those days was that shops would give you a deposit back for any glass bottles that you took them. So, Malcolm and I had a little enterprise of collecting bottles when and wherever we could find them. We would store them in his dad's shed until we had enough that would buy us both a Mars bar or bottle of pop. Different bottles were worth different amounts so we would have it all worked out before we took them to the shop just what we would be able to buy. It was a great moment taking them back aside from the job of acquiring the bottles from our parents or hedgerows. We felt that we had got our sweets and pop for free. I remember after one such transaction taking our pop and sweets down to the factory. There was a field at the side where they put scrap machinery from the factory. There was all manner of bits of wagons and metalwork for us to hide amongst to eat and drink our booty, and as we sat and gorged ourselves we noticed a barrel-like milk tank from the back of a wagon laying on the ground across the way. So, after we finished our sweets we went over to have a look. At one end there was a hatch which would offer us a look inside but it was too high, but after pushing the round tank a bit the hatch came low enough for us to open and have a look inside. There was a pristine stainless steel interior which we just had to investigate, so after each of us climbed in feet first we found ourselves in this smooth slippery cylinder with our voices echoing off the sides. We now found if one climbed up the side the tank would roll a bit and make the other lose their balance, so it quickly became a game of knocking each other off their feet and sliding down the sides. This went on for some time till we felt that this fairground ride was over and we managed to clamber our way out. It's only now looking back that I can see the danger we put ourselves in with the risk of the door closing on us. We seemed to live a charmed life with the potential for accidents in a lot of the things we did.

There was one day when from the return of bottles we had worked out we would have enough for fish and chips from Watson's fish shop in the village. A fish was a shilling and chips were sixpence which would be seven and a half pence today. We would have told our mothers what we were going to do as we wouldn't have needed our evening tea. The fish shop was run by my half cousins' mum and dad, Mavis and Cyril. Mum had bought us fish and chips from there in the past but this was the first time either of us had been on our own. Malcolm got served first and paid with his bottle money, then when I got mine and tried to pay, Uncle Cyril, as I would call him, winked at me and told me to keep my money for another day. I was amazed to get fish and chips for free, something Malcolm couldn't believe either. However, when I told Mum she said I shouldn't make a habit of going as she obviously didn't want me to test Uncle Cyril's generosity.

Remains of the swimming pool at Givendale

Dad and Lance putting up the roof on the Nissan hut

Grandma & Grandad Harding.

Me and my brothers & sisters in our front garden

Chapter 5

It would be around the beginning of April and I was going to go with Dad to pick up some calves in the van. It was around an hour and a half drive away so Dad had made some partitions in the back of the van to help keep the calves comfortable and safe. These would be a new type of animal to the farm so I was looking forward to seeing them. Some pigs had been moved from the barn to the Nissen hut to make way for them. Dad had built some small pens for them and bought some new buckets to feed them with too. We had set off early as Dad wanted to get them back to the barn as soon as he could to get them settled into their new surroundings. Often when Dad would travel anywhere in the pick-up or van he would take a mug of tea with him which he would place on the floor. I would look at the mug and then at Dad as he would slowly drive down the lane. I was always surprised how little spilled out which always made Dad smile, but today as we were going further we had a flask and some sandwiches. It was a cold day and the van heater didn't seem to make much difference as there was no separate cab on the van.It would have to heat up all the back of the van too, so we both had coats on as we headed out. I don't ever remember Dad having a map but he seemed to know where he was going. There weren't many motorways around then so we were on A and B roads all the way. The journey started out straightforward enough but after about an hour we started to near the Pennines. I don't remember exactly where we picked the calves up from but it was certainly hilly, and as soon as we neared the hills it started to snow. It quickly became heavy wet snow and almost immediately the wipers stopped working so Dad had to slide the door open and clear the windscreen with his hand until he could find somewhere to pull off the road. After he pulled over he had a go at fixing them but to no avail. So, as it didn't look as if it was going to clear any time soon, and not wanting to drive on snowy roads if it started to settle, Dad pressed on periodically clearing snow from the windscreen with his hand.

What should have been another twenty minutes took about an hour and eventually we pulled into the farmyard. It didn't take too long to load up the calves and thankfully by then the snow had eased off somewhat and there wasn't too much on the road. If the weather hadn't eased we would have set off straightaway, but as it was we had a sandwich and a cup of tea before setting off.

So, we were more relaxed now as we headed off back home. The one thing I hadn't imagined was the noise that the calves would make. They really did make a racket as their bellowing bounced around the back of the van. They were certainly missing their mothers and I wondered whether I was going to enjoy having calves around if they were going to be this noisy. But at least the weather was a little better and the roads dried out as we got away from the hills. The rest of the journey was uneventful and Jenny and Alison were in the stackyard to greet us as we arrived back safe and sound.

Dad let the girls have a quick look at the calves before making preparations to put them in their new home. Each calf had its own pen made with sheep hurdles with a bed of straw in each. Dad had to carry each calf one by one to the pens, still bellowing their hearts out. He said he would feed them to hopefully calm them down a bit. They were still on milk but it was a special powdered milk which had to be mixed with warm water. Each bucket had to have a measured amount which he then had to get one of the calves to drink before it went cold. As drinking out of a bucket isn't natural he had to train them, which he did by first getting the calf to suck his fingers then put his hand with the calf still sucking into the bucket of milk, eventually getting the calf to suck the milk instead of his fingers. This proved to be a lengthy process as one instinct the calves have is to lift their head up quickly to release more milk from the udder. Of course, if they do this with their head in a bucket and you're not holding tight then it's a bucket of milk wasted. Dad fed them all himself that afternoon and for the next day or so but then let me help him when I could. My sisters and myself had already taken to popping into the barn to get the calves to suck our fingers which was good fun but a bit mean on the calves as they thought they were going to be fed. Helping to feed the calves was okay, if only they didn't butt and move about so much. It really was a bit of a wrestle with milk splashing about, for me anyway. However, once they were used to the buckets the buckets could be fastened to the pen making it a lot easier and it was surprising how quickly they grew.

It was fairly rare that I got into trouble with Mum and Dad aside from the fertiliser bag incident and playing with matches. I wasn't too bad so it came as a bit of a surprise when one day Mum accused me of shooting her clothes pegs off the clothes line for most of the washing to fall to the ground. I have to admit that I had once shot a couple of pegs off the line for target practice, but I'm sure it was Dad that first instigated it and even then it was only a few and they weren't holding washing up at the time. Plus, the air rifle pellets broke them and I had disposed of the evidence. Anyway, no matter how much I protested my innocence the blame still lay with me.

There was however one instance that got me into the most serious trouble that I ever caused my parents. It started one afternoon when Paul and I were out and about when a light aircraft caught our attention as it kept circling around us. We ended up laying on our backs watching it at which point Paul started to make up a fanciful story about what it was up to. He said the plane was full of secret agents and that they had come to spy on us. No sooner had he finished speaking two people jumped out of it. We jumped to our feet in amazement as these two bodies fell towards the ground before two parachutes opened. They drifted down and away from us to disappear behind woodland in the distance. We had never seen anything like this before and ran back to the farm to tell my dad, who was perhaps too busy to take too much interest so we returned to our secret agent theories. No more light was shed on the incident and Paul later left for his tea. I too had my tea and sometime later was near the railway line near the edge of our property when a group of lads from the village came by. I did know some of them but they were all older than me. They said they were on their way to the Seaton Ross show by cutting across the fields at the other side of the railway. I had never heard of the Seaton Ross show and they asked me if I wanted to go with them. I said I'd better ask Mum and Dad but it quickly became a man or a mouse thing and I either went with them now or not at all because they weren't going to wait. So, to save face I said okay and tagged along. It was quite a long way and I wouldn't have been able to find my way back on my own, so once there I had to stay till they went back.

Seaton Ross is only a small village but had an annual show and of course it turned out that the skydivers had been part of it. There was a small fairground which was the reason the lads from Holme had come. I hadn't brought any money but the lads seemed happy to look after me and pay for a ride here and there. It was dark before we made our way back and luckily there was a bit of moonlight as no one had a torch. As we set off I realised that I was going to be way later than I had ever been leaving either Paul's or Malcolm's. Now that I knew how far it was I knew Mum and Dad wouldn't have let me go if I had asked them, and it now began to dawn on me that I was going to be in trouble as it was eleven pm as I entered the stackyard. When I saw Dad standing outside near the veranda I feared the worst. They had rung the Rosses and the Simpsons and anyone else they could think of and were getting to the point of ringing the police. I got a proper dressing down and the term being grounded wasn't in use back then but that's effectively what happened. For the next week I hung around the farm helping out where I could in an effort to get back in their good books. There were the usual jobs of helping to feed the animals and putting new bedding down.

But towards the weekend Dad, Grandad, Garth and Gordon Fox had cut a two acre field of corn by hand with scythes. The field belonged to the Moors at the other side of the railway line who had let Dad grow some barley in it. However, when it came to combining it the combine couldn't get into the field so it all had to be cut by hand and stooked up. At the weekend Dad had arranged for the combine to come to the farm and the rest of us would load the four-wheel trailer up with the stooks. We would then take the trailer to the combine parked in a clear part of one of our fields and feed the stooks into the front of the combine with pitchforks. So, while Gordon and Garth finished off stooking I drove the tractor and four-wheel trailer with Grandad on the back and Dad would load the stooks on the trailer with a pitchfork. The stooks were put together in groups across the field, so I would drive to a group and Dad would throw them up to Grandad who would stack them, then I would drive to the next group and so on. Easy enough for me to start with but as the trailer got heavier and with the ground being a little soft I had to give the tractor a little more throttle to set off, and I remember setting off one time with a bit of a jolt and looking back to see Grandad having to steady himself with his pitchfork before looking at me and then pointing at me with a wry smile on his face. Once the trailer was full it was a steady drive across the railway line (which Dad did) to the combine where they were then fed into the combine. Quite a lengthy process but at the end of it Dad would have his own store of corn. He had decided to buy a milling machine to mill his own corn which would save money in the long run.

The railway was closing down and the last freight train had passed and they would soon be taking up the track. So, there would be no more collecting coal with Grandad and no more trains for Brandy to chase. It would be sad not to see the passing steam trains anymore. It didn't matter what I was doing when a steam train passed, I would always take the time to watch its energy. They were impossible to ignore if you were up close; the steam, the smoke, the sound and the movement were captivating and I would miss them.

The Vespa scooter used by Garth and Lance had broken and wasn't being used anymore and was languishing in one of the sheds. The splines on the kick-start were rounded off for one thing and who knows what else was wrong. It wasn't something we had paid any mind to and it had been there for quite a few weeks now, but one day for whatever reason it caught both Paul's and my attention and we decided to have a look. Of course, we knew little about engines and Dad didn't have the time and wasn't interested in trying to get it going, so we took to messing about with it anyway to see if we could fathom something out. We knew it started with a kick-start so we tried to fix that first. With the few tools we had we tightened it back on as tight as we could but it soon slipped round again as we tried to kick it off. I'm sure Garth and Lance must have already tried this before but the thought of getting it going was strong so we persevered till we realised it wouldn't matter how tight we fitted it on as it would still slip round. We had a look at the engine but of course we didn't know how it really worked, so in the end we would push it down the stackyard and take it in turns to sit on and steer it until it tired us both out and we would put it back in the shed for another day.

Jenny, Alison and myself were on our way with Dad to Boggle House on Howden Road which is where Grandad lives with his sister Aunty Polly as we called her. Aunty Polly was a fairly small grey-haired woman who always had her hair tied in a bob towards the back of her head. She usually had an apron or pinny on with a long black or dark dress and black lace-up boots. She reminded me of Mary Poppins and she always made a fuss when we visited, wanting to get us tea and cake and enquire what we had been up to. The house was detached and stood on two and a half acres of land. Inside was very old fashioned with different chairs with knitted throws, old solid wood chests of drawers and the walls had old dark pictures of horses and animals in farm stackyards. There were a number of other picture portraits that faded out to a black surround. I'm not sure if they were pictures of relatives or not. The kitchen had a stone sink with cold water tap, a couple of free-standing cupboards and a pantry in the corner which was the fridge of the day. The windows weren't very big so it was quite dark inside and if the room fell silent all you could hear was the loud ticking of their clock. They had no television, just a wireless on a chest of drawers, so Grandad's evening entertainment would sometimes be at the pub just down the road. Outside were a couple of outbuildings one of which had a chemical toilet in, again with the strong smell of Jeyes Fluid. We wouldn't stay all that long, just enough time to have a chat and a cup of tea and cake. Before we left we would each get a Nuttall's Mintoe to take with us. Looking back Grandad seemed to live a simple life as I don't remember him going on holiday anywhere, but he was known by many in the village and always had time for people and seemed happy.

Mr Wilson had organised another camping trip, this time it was to the Lake District, which would be the furthest away that we had camped so far. It was too far to be going in the back of an army wagon so we were going by coach. The usual preparations and packing had been done and this time Andrew Macphearson was coming with us. After loading up and setting off from the scout hut – for some reason which I can't remember we went down the back roads through Everingham towards Melbourne – we turned from Melbourne towards Pocklington. We had to go over a humpback bridge that crossed the Pocklington canal and just as the coach got to the top of the hump something broke and it stopped dead on the top blocking the road. It was something reasonably serious that wasn't going to be fixed with a quick look under the bonnet, so when this was realised we all got off the bus for a walk along the canal. Even getting a mechanic took some time as someone had to walk back into Melbourne to the phone box, so it was going to be an hour or two at best before we were off again. I can remember walking past the lock and then along the side of the canal which was lined with brick and stepped down into the crystal-clear water. Then as we looked deeper into the canal we could see numerous perch clearly as they swam along. We had a good walk along the canal and back spending the remaining time sat on the bank side until the coach had been fixed. Once the coach had been repaired we climbed back aboard and back on our way to the Lake District. We were heading for a farm west of Windermere near Hawkshead Hill. With the delay we of course arrived later than we had planned, but as we had all now camped before it didn't take as long to set up as the last camp. The field we were camping in was on a slope and had a small brook that ran down the side, so we made sure the tents were positioned across the slope so we didn't all roll into each other during the night. We did the usual collection of wood for the fires and then set about cooking our evening meal. It wasn't until we had eaten and tidied things away that we had a chance to have a proper look at our site. Behind us the slope grew into quite a steep incline to what looked like a substantial hill beyond, but in front of us we were looking down on classic Lake District scenery with glimpses of Lake Windermere and the mountain tops in the distance. We were surrounded by sheep again so would have their periodic bleating to help us sleep, although the brook that ran down the slope was quite rocky so made quite a bit of noise. In spite of us being late we still had time for our evening sing song in the main tent with "Ging gang goolie goolie watcha ging gang goo" and "My bonnie lies over the ocean" being two of them. Mr Wilson also outlined some of the activities that we would be attempting during the week. Our two sixers would each be making a bivouac that they would have to sleep in and one day we would all take part in orienteering, but as it had been a long day we were all now ready to retire to our tents. I will never tire of waking from a night in a tent and then emerge from its confines into a beautiful sunny morning with wonderful views and just the muffled sounds of some of the rest of our crew as they too stir from their tents. Of course, not all mornings would be like this but this was July and we were having a good run of hot sunny days. After a quick wash fires had to be lit as we always started the day with bacon and eggs and a mug of tea. Water had to be carried from the farm quite some distance away which made it a bit of a chore as the clear plastic containers we had to carry the water seemed to get heavier and heavier the further you went. After breakfast the two sixers were going to make a start on their bivouacs which they would sleep in tonight. They were going to build them in the small woodland nearby. First they would build a frame out of dead branches, nothing too big, just big enough to get in with your sleeping bag, then they would add more sticks, enough to support either grass sods or leaf litter depending on the time of year and what was available. Also, they would have to light their own fires and cook their own food.

The rest of us would go on a small hike to check out the lie of the land and see what was around. So, after all was tidy and we had filled a couple of packs with some snacks and water we headed off up the hill behind us. Each group had an ordnance survey map and compass so we could map our journey. After about an hour we had made it to the top of the hill behind us to find quite a big body of water which was called Tarn Hows that looked really nice and clear. Mr Wilson said that tomorrow we could come up and have a swim there which we all looked forward to.

We next plotted a circular route back to camp on the map which we then had to follow using points of reference like streams, contours and hedgerows to keep to our route. It was just a small test of our map reading skills for future orienteering trips, something I enjoyed and was a bit like working out a puzzle. We took our time as we followed our route with Mr Wilson quizzing us on tree types, shrubs and bird species as we went along. After stopping for a break we made it back to camp a few hours later and had a stop by the woodland to see how the lads had got on with their bivouac building. They were just putting the final touches to them and had used grass sods to cover them which would give cover but would be interesting if they were to get heavy rain. However, with the weather we were having they would have a cosy night. Mr Wilson had arranged a game for us to play as evening neared. He had marked out an area either side of a bridge that crossed the brook that someone had to defend as well as the bridge while the rest had to try and enter these areas and light a banger, not a game a scoutmaster these days would dream of or get away with playing. But this being the sixties off we went. We had a piece of wool tied round our arms which if the defender pulled off took us out of the game.

I don't remember too much about the battle that ensued. I remember Andrew Macphearson being the formidable defender and I remember the whistle blowing signalling the end of the game as darkness fell. We all made our way to stoke up the campfire to finish the evening with a sing song and had all been sat around the fire for some time when all of a sudden the sound of a banger rang out. We all looked at each other at which point we realised that Richard Towse or "trout" as he was called wasn't with us. He hadn't heard the whistle and was still playing the game which we all found hilarious and fell about laughing. At the end of the evening Andrew and Steven made their way to their bivouacs as we retired to our tents.

We arose in the morning to another dry sunny day so the lads did have an easy night in their bivouacs. The good weather makes everything so much easier from lighting fires to sitting and eating outside. Today we would be going swimming which we were all looking forward to, but that wouldn't be until later in the afternoon. In the meantime we had water to fetch, wood to collect and field studies putting different knots to use and the like. I don't remember disliking anything that we did. Before we could head off up to Tarn Hows Mr Wilson decided we should prepare our evening meal first. We were having mincemeat so while someone lit the fire I was chopping onions ready to fry off and the meat was put into a tall deep pot that would hang from the tripod. Once the fire was ready the onions were fried off and the meat was hung over the fire. Vegetables were prepared and put in pans of water but wouldn't be cooked until we got back. Then Mr Wilson dropped the bombshell and asked me if I would stay behind and look after the meat. We all had great respect for Mr Wilson so didn't question his wishes, but inside I was devastated and could only look up the hill longingly as they all disappeared over the ridge and out of sight. Because there was a lot of meat in the pot it needed constant stirring and adjustment on the fire so as not to burn it.

Eventually though the meat was cooked and the fire had died down to just a few red embers. Although I had been told to stay back and tend the meat it wasn't clear whether I was to stay behind the whole time, so I decided the meat would be fine now and if I ran up the hill I could join them for the last part of the swim. So that's what I did. I grabbed my gear and tore off up to the Tarn. When I got there they had all swum out to an island about sixty yards out so I was straight in and swam out to join them. Mr Wilson did look a little surprised to see me but just asked if all was well which I assured him it was.

It was great to swim with your friends in hot sunshine in clear water with no chlorine to sting your eyes. We spent another half hour or more enjoying the swim before heading back. We were all still buzzing with the day's activity as our campsite came into view, when someone pointed out that two of the green tents were now black, which indeed they were. We were now all transfixed with what had caused two of the tents to turn black and it wasn't until we were about ten feet away that we could see the reason. They were both completely covered in flying ants. It was unbelievable, two four-man tents were completely covered with them. None of us including Mr Wilson had ever seen anything like it and weren't quite sure what to do about it. We were still pondering what to do when we noticed that the tripod with the pot of meat was laying on the ground. It looked like a dog had knocked it over and eaten half of it. As soon as I saw what had happened I wanted a hole in the ground to swallow me up. I could feel the eyes of everyone staring at me although nothing was said. I think Mr Wilson could see how mortified I was. Attention though was soon back to the flying ants which seemed to take the sting out of my misdemeanour, but as it happened the ants simply flew away as quickly as they had arrived. The rest of the camping trip was perhaps less eventful but just as enjoyable and we had good weather the whole week. Andrew and Steven got their bivouac badges and we all managed to fit in another swim back in the Tarn. The coach didn't miss a beat and delivered us safely home. At the time we took for granted the work of our cub and scoutmasters, but now looking back we can really appreciate the time that they gave to give us the experiences and times that we had.

The fair had come to the village and had set up on the piece of land near to Grandad's house. It was always one of the highlights of the year and generated a good turnout of villagers. It had the usual hook a duck, coconut shy and numerous other side stalls, but the star of the event was the waltzer and the speedway. The waltzer always made me feel ill so I would only watch people on it, however the speedway was the ride to be on. It's a very benign ride these days with some of the rides they have now, but back then it was a macho ride that any lad worth his salt would want to be seen on, sat astride a motorbike as it made its way round to the sound of stirring sixties music of the day. We always marvelled at the lads that ran the attraction as they casually got on and off the fast-moving ride.

I had been with Mum and Dad to Hull Fair before which I remember had a lot of scary side stalls with someone in a cage that would turn into a gorilla with the help of strange music, flashing lights and smoke. But our village fair only had the traditional stalls. This was the first year that I had been allowed to go on my own or at least with friends. I went with Andrew Macphearson who I remember seemed to have endless money to spend. On the other hand Paul had a more businesslike approach to the fair that he thankfully shared with me. He would wait for the fair to pack up and leave, then first thing the following morning he would call round and we would ride down to the empty field where it had been sited. At first I wondered why we were here but as we began to crawl around in the grass, especially where the waltzer and speedway had been, I realised why. We began to find money. It was unbelievable, not just pennies but threepenny bits, sixpences, shillings and Paul even found a half crown, a true case of finders keepers, so it was sweets and pop on the way home with plenty for another day. I was of course sworn to secrecy as he wanted us to keep it to ourselves. Another annual event was the gymkhana which was primarily about horses and ponies, but was also run as an annual show with tents full of different types of work entered by children from the village and surrounding area. Jenny was still too young to enter any of the races or jumps but entered a sort of best dressed pony and rider which Mum helped with. Another thing we entered was to build a miniature garden using a mirror to simulate a pond, then we used sand and all manner of things to create flowerbeds and shrubs which again we built with a little help from Mother. I can still remember the moment when we were able to check on our entries after the judging to see a red rosette and certificate on our entry. It's quite amazing how such a small prize would excite children as they realised they have won a prize, whether it was first or third didn't really matter as to see a rosette of any colour was a win and something to treasure, for a while at least.

We had even more excitement too when Jenny won a rosette in the best dressed pony and rider.

The village had a well built and well used village hall with a football field and cricket pitch behind, and periodically they would put up a big screen and show a Disney film. All the chairs were stacked up round the outside of the hall and we would take a chair and place it in a row to sit on. But Malcolm and myself liked to get there early because the hall had a highly polished floor and the chairs were made from bent metal tubing. So, we found if you pushed the chair quickly across the floor and jumped on the chair would glide across the floor a good distance. Of course, we could only do this while the hall was still empty and before anyone told us to stop. When all had settled down and we were all sitting on our chairs the entertainment would start with cartoons before the main picture.

One night Mum had left me with Jenny and Alison and the film we were going to watch was *The Wizard of Oz*. Everyone enjoyed the cartoons and most of the film, but when it came to the part where you hear the sound of the wizard a ripple of fear went through the audience possibly started by Alison. Before the wizard had stopped talking there were tears and many could take no more and one of those was Alison. So right there and then I had to take Alison and Jenny out along with other crying children scurrying through the door. And that was the end of the film for them and me also. It would be quite some time before I finally saw the end of *The Wizard of Oz*.

I had another go at the Vespa scooter today. Malcolm was round and he had seen his dad take out the spark plug on their lawnmower and clean it with a piece of sandpaper when their mower wouldn't start, so that became our task and with the help of a screwdriver and adjustable spanner we managed to take a side panel off and remove the spark plug. Then with the help of Mum's nail file we scraped and cleaned the plug as best we could. We felt sure this was the answer as to us the plug did look dirty, so with great expectation we had the plug put back in and panel back on and were ready for ignition. We both pushed it along then I quickly jumped on and put it into gear as

Malcolm kept pushing. Alas, we ground to a halt without it firing, but we wouldn't give up so this time Malcolm would jump on while I kept pushing. Again we came to a halt and despite a few further attempts we had no luck and had to retire the scooter once again to its home in the shed.

One evening while we were having tea Mum told us about something she had seen. The washing line is behind a hedge next to the orchard and can't be seen from the house. She said that when she had gone to bring in the washing and went through the gap in the hedge she could see clothes on the ground, then as she looked further along the washing line she saw Baldry's parrot systematically shuffling along the line and unclipping the pegs with its beak making a very thorough job of it with only a couple of pegs missed. It seemed to have it down to a fine art and must have done this to other washing lines in the neighbourhood. I didn't get an apology but at least we knew who the phantom washing line fiend was.

I was going to stay the night at Andrew Macphearson's and one of the things we were going to do was build an Airfix model of the SS *Canberra*, a cruise ship with swimming pools on the top deck, something we hadn't seen before. We had one each and were going to build them together at the same time. Andrew had a younger sister called Ann and I remember his dad having quite a strong Scottish accent which was stronger still when he would tell Andrew off for not flushing the toilet. "Andrew, will you please remember to flush the toilet, your wee wee has acid in it and will stain the bowl," I remember him saying which I don't think would have been the first time he had told Andrew. Airfix model building was relatively easy but Andrew showed me magazines that he had and a model building pack which showed you how to design a car and make a prototype out of clay using special tools to shave and fashion the clay. Even back then some of the designs looked very futuristic. He said it was something he was going to do but was way out of my capabilities, and I would be sticking to Airfix models for now. Andrew was only a year older than me but was a very clever lad and had views and an understanding of the world that was way beyond me. He knew all the main politicians of the day and their positions and numerous other things that I had no understanding of and couldn't hope to even comment on. If we had watched a film together for the first time, hours later or even days later he would be able to reel off scenes from the film word for word, something that amazed me at the time. In some ways he was in a different world to me but we still had plenty of common interests which kept the friendship going. I remember working on the Airfix models late into the evening and getting very tired as I would normally be in bed by about nine o'clock, but Andrew said he didn't normally go to bed until about eleven or half past and explained why. He had it pointed out to him that if you lived to be seventy-five you had been asleep for twenty-five years, at work or school for about twenty-five years, six months in traffic jams, six months looking for keys etc, etc. So, he had decided to cut back on his sleep to at least pinch back a bit of time to do other things. Whilst the idea was a bit of an eye opener for me it didn't move me to make any changes, certainly not with my sleep patterns anyway.

In the morning I learned of at least one difference between the Scottish and the English. At breakfast they asked if I would like some porridge which I said I did. As I took my first mouthful they saw the look on my face as the taste of salt hit my taste buds. They of course explained that that was how they had porridge in Scotland and would get me something else. It's funny looking back how foreign the concept of salt in porridge was. At the time I thought they had made a mistake and couldn't believe that they preferred it like that. Sometime before I went home Mr Macphearson was proud to show me their Renault car which he was cleaning and in particular the Zeibart damp proofing that he'd had done. I remember thinking at the time that it wouldn't be something my dad would ever dream of having done to any of his vehicles. Mr Macphearson was great with us, was always engaging, and would take us places and pick us up if needed.

Paul with Steven and Richard keeping an eye on the piglets.

Steven & Richard with the old Bedford van

Steven in wheel barrow near the lean to building that Paul and I nearly set fire to.

Horses in front garden, Steven on Brough

Steven & Richard on their bike, with their home-made helmets

Chapter 6

The demolition of the railway was in full swing and we had seen freight trains loaded with track and wooden railway sleepers pass by periodically, until eventually they were working on the track near the farm. A train with a crane and flat carriages was moving along one track while taking the other track at the side up. I watched some of the men on the track knocking out the clips and other men with two-handed wrenches undoing the bolts of the fittings that held the track in place. Within a few days they had disappeared from view with just one track left to take up. Then one day when I came home from school there was an empty open-topped goods wagon sitting on the track, the sort of wagon that would carry coal or stone. After I had my tea I went down to have a look. All was quiet with any workers having finished for the day so I climbed up to have a look inside to see that it was empty. After pondering what to do I had a ride into the village to see who was about. There was no one near the school so I went to the village hall. There I found some of my friends from school playing football and told them what I had found and asked if anyone wanted to join me to see if we could move it. They all seemed intrigued and duly stowed the football and joined me on their bikes. On our way we rounded up a few more until there were fourteen of us in all.

We went down Holly Lane and then along the side of the railway to the crossing near to where the wagon was. We all left our bikes near the crossing and then scrambled along the railway to the wagon. Everyone found a place to climb up the wagon to have a look, and as we all peered in we hatched a plan. Seven would get in and the other seven would push, so just like picking football teams we divided ourselves up and seven climbed all the way in while the rest climbed back down. We elected to push it away from the crossing which was possibly our only thought on safety, so we positioned ourselves around the back of the wagon and began to push. It took quite an effort to get it moving but before long we were pushing almost as fast as we could run, at which point instead of letting go someone climbed on which led everyone else to do the same. We all climbed over and into the wagon with the rest. The wagon trundled along making the classic "dun, dun, dun, dun" as it went over the joints in the track. It was surprising how far it went before it slowly ground to a halt, then it was the turn of the other seven.

We all found it an exciting and unique experience, probably helped in part with us working as a team similar to football. We must have gone half a mile or more before we decided we had better start to push it back before we ran out of energy. I remember getting back and all standing together on the track, some with their hands on their knees catching their breath and laughing as we recounted the event. Someone had tripped and fallen just as the rest started to climb aboard. He didn't hurt himself but had everyone else shouting that he would miss the train as he ran to catch up. And that was my last ever experience of the railway as far as trains and track were concerned. I never saw them take up the remaining track. One day after school I wandered down to check things out and it had gone, just a long empty uneven surface where the sleepers had been. No more Stop, Look, and Listen and no more steam trains to turn your head.

Our dog Brandy was like another member of the family like many dogs are, but with us living on a farm she had the freedom to do what she wanted. We never took her for a walk. I don't know if we even had a dog lead. She would sleep in the house at night and be out with Dad in the morning and would be free to come and go as she pleased, although she never went beyond our property unless it was down the railway line with Dad and I shooting. She would usually meet us when we came back from school but she was always in the background. She never made a great fuss of anyone except perhaps Dad. You would never get her to fetch a ball or stick or anything like that, it was as if she was above that and had more sense. She was a guard dog and would keep an eye on any new faces but as I said never bit anyone, but I'm sure would have done to anyone who showed aggression towards us. She had an open wound at the top of her left leg which she'd had for a number of years which nobody could fix, so she and we had learned to live with it. The back door would be open all the time and would be late in the evening, the summer especially, before it was closed, so it wasn't unusual for Brandy to still be outside late on. But one night when she wasn't in I thought maybe the door was closed and she was locked out and went to check. The door was open so I wandered outside to have a look. She was down on her belly in the middle of the stackyard with her head on her paws. I shouted for her to come but she didn't move so I went over to see what was wrong. Again, I told her to come as I got close. She didn't move but just moved her eyes to look at me. At that point I realised something was wrong and put my arms under her to help her to her feet. She could barely stand so I took some of her weight as I helped her towards the house. I started to shout for Dad as she inched along and hadn't gone too far before he came outside. There were tears in my eyes as I told Dad there's something wrong with Brandy. Dad picked her up and took her inside. Soon everyone had gathered round wanting to comfort her and Mum got her a drink of water but she wouldn't drink it. We spent some time in relative silence with Dad sitting by her side stroking her while fielding questions from my brothers and sisters. Eventually Mum decided we should all go to bed. Before I went upstairs Dad had opened a bottle of beer and put it in her bowl and she was licking some of it up. I asked Dad if that would make her better to which he replied we will see. Next morning I was up early to check on Brandy. Her bed was empty and for a second I thought she must be okay and outside somewhere as usual, until I saw Mum and Dad's faces as they looked at each other and then me which said it all. Dad didn't say that she had died, he said she had gone, but I knew what that meant and quickly burst into tears. It was of course a sad time for all for a while. I guess Dad must have buried her somewhere on the farm and wasn't something that was ever talked about. Brandy though would never be forgotten.

The riding of Brough for me had become something of a chore, and while I liked Brough, who had become a very reliable and friendly pony, to ride him most days to give him exercise was something I looked forward to less and less. We had plenty of nice stables but we had no fenced paddock to put him in, so I would have to take him out most days around or across the fields depending on what was in the field. Some days Dad or Grandad would take him out with Jenny or Alison on which would give me a break. One day I took him out and had ridden him round the fields and had arrived back at the farm and was going to put him back in the stable when Dad told me to give him a good gallop across the field and back. So, I turned him and galloped across the field, turned at the other end and galloped back to Dad which made him smile. "Go on," he said, "give him another run," so off again I went across the field and was about three quarters of the way back when something blowing in the hedgerow made the pony suddenly change direction and I fell off. It was cultivated soil so was reasonably soft so at first when I got up I thought all was okay, but then I felt pain in my right elbow and looked to see my arm bent round at a funny angle from my elbow. I then began to run towards Dad shouting, "Dad, Dad, Dad, my arm, my arm, my arm!" He quickly put my arm back across my stomach, picked me up and carried me back to the house. I was still feeling sick and faint as we set off in the car to hospital. At the hospital they told Dad he shouldn't have put the arm back, which I wasn't too sure about. I don't think I would have been too happy about going all the way to hospital with my arm all twisted. However, no bones were broken but they said it would have to be in a sling for a few months which would get me out of doing chores for a while. I wouldn't be going to school for some time either so would spend my time helping Mum entertain and keep an eye on Steven and Richard.

Over the next few weeks I developed some really impressive bruising which I would show everyone whether they wanted to see it or not. Another thing that was happening around that time was our field of peas was going to be harvested, which back then involved a gang of people from the village coming to pull the pea vines by hand then pull the pods from the vines and put them into a net. The nets would hold around four stones of peapods which would take some time to fill. Once full you would take them to the scales to be weighed where you would receive a few shillings for each netful. So, it would be predominantly women that came with just a few men, but also children would come to help their mothers fill the nets. It was quite a family affair and an annual event that I liked to help out with. It had been about three weeks now since my accident and whilst I perhaps shouldn't be taking part in the pea harvest, I was determined not to miss out. It was as much a social event as it was a job of work with plenty of conversation and banter over the sound of the squeak of pods being pulled from the vine. I found that I could pull the vines up with my left arm and then with my right arm still in the sling hold a vine and strip the pods off with my left arm. It was a lot slower than I would normally be but at least I was able to take part and earn a bit of money too.

Over the next few weeks, I was able to take off my sling but found that I couldn't straighten my arm, so after going to physio I had to perform a daily task of lifting something of a certain weight three times a day, which in my case was a pouffe, a cushioned footstool we had that had a cord around it that I could hold to lift it several times. This of course went on for weeks and weeks until my arm was as straight as it was ever going to be and things could get back to normal.

I was going with Andrew Macphearson to York on the bus, not something I would have done on my own at nine years old or with any other friend for that matter, but even though Andrew was only ten he had that air of confidence and fearlessness that meant I was happy that he would get us there and back safely. We were going to take the two Roman coins that Dad and I had found to York Museum to find any information we could about them, not least if they were worth anything. As we took our seats on the bus and purchased our tickets Andrew told the ticket collector where we wanted to go in York and he said he would make sure we got off at the right stop. That alone put me at ease as I had never even been to

91

York before let alone on the bus. Andrew too had never been on the bus to York but had been with his parents before in the car, so did know a little about York's layout.

The journey to York took around an hour and the ticket collector made sure we got off at the right stop, however when Andrew saw Clifford's Tower he knew we should be getting off there. Before we got off Andrew asked where we should go to catch the bus back, which was just the other side of the road and would have Market Weighton on it, so now we knew how to get home. The museum isn't far at all from the tower so we were soon at the entrance asking at the ticket office if there was anyone that could tell us anything about the Roman coins. They said they would see and asked us to wait at the side. It wasn't long before a really nice gentleman came to see us and we showed him the coins. He seemed quite enthusiastic about them and said he would take them with him to do a bit of research on them, and in the meantime we could have a look round the museum if we liked and he would find us when he had some information. We thought that was great to be able to have a look round the museum for free as Andrew hadn't been before either. The museum was great for a couple of young lads with different streets set out as they would have been years before, and we managed to have a good rake around for about an hour before the gentleman found us with news on the coins. He took us to a glass display case where he laid out some paperwork and then took out the two coins from a fancy little envelope that they had put them in. He then told us in detail all about the coins, the dates and who was depicted on them. It was all very interesting, especially when he told us they were two thousand years old. However, what we really wanted to know was if they were worth anything. We were conscious of being too keen on asking how much they might be worth and had even discussed with each other how we would tackle the question, but in the end we needn't have worried as towards the end of the information he was giving he said in spite of their age they aren't really worth anything. This was of course disappointing but we had information about them, a nice envelope and a free look round the museum. After we thanked the man for his help

Andrew said we had time for a quick run round York centre with our first port of call being the top of the hill that Clifford's Tower is perched on. Then from there we made our way to Marks and Spencer having a quick look on every floor before going out of a back door into a market. He then showed me the shambles which were similar to the streets in the museum, before we made our way back more or less the way we had come to catch the bus home. It had been a great day for me being the first time I had been in a department store and experienced the hustle and bustle of a city centre. I had a lot to tell Mum and Dad when I got back.

I had driven the tractor many times by now but usually with a trailer on the back and hadn't actually done any major work with it, but that was about to change as Dad said it was time I had a go at ploughing. I was going to plough our smallest field next to the railway or former railway as it was now. Dad watched over me as I backed up to the plough to yolk it up to the tractor. I had watched and helped Dad to yolk up to this and other machinery before so I knew how everything worked, but of course inching the tractor backwards, lowering the arms and making sure you were square all at the same time wasn't quite as easy as I thought. Dad though was calm and patient and with a few words of correction we were connected up. He told me to drive onto the headland where he showed me how to set it up, then we walked along the headland and he told me how to mark out the field ploughing it in a series of ratchets. The field was triangular so there would be a lot of short turns later on, but for now after I had marked out my first ratchet Dad followed me as I made the first run up and down. He made a few alterations telling me what he was doing and why, and then that was it. He left me to it. I was soon in my own little world concentrating on keeping straight and making sure all was working properly. Then as time went by I found myself trying to make the turns at the end smoother which would help later on as the turns got shorter and shorter. The field was only a couple of acres but all the short turns made it seem a lot bigger, not that it mattered to me. I was in my element and loved every minute and would bore anyone, friend or family, with the achievement for weeks to come.

There were a number of smaller scout camping trips that I went on, but the last week-long camp that I remember well was one where we went to Lealholm north east of Pickering in north Yorkshire. We had again travelled by coach and were met by a tractor and trailer on the north side of the River Esk in Lealholm where we had to transfer all the gear from the bus to the trailer as the farm track was a bit rough. After the trailer was loaded it started to make its way down the farm track and we all followed behind on foot. We went about a mile and a half before the tractor turned to cross the river via a ford, the field we were camping in being a relatively flat field just the other side of the river. We crossed the river using some stepping stones at the side of the ford and began the job of setting up camp. Again there were sixteen of us so we had four tents to put up as well as the main tent. Wood for the fires had to be collected from a small woodland on the other side of the river and water too had to be carried from the farm six hundred yards or so at the other side as well.

During our evening meeting in the main tent Mr Wilson told us that each group would be making a raft one of the days which we would then race against each other, something that had us all looking at each other. We would also be doing some fishing which we knew about as we had all brought some fishing gear. Also, there would be the usual field studies at various points. So, as we went to bed that night the talk was all about raft building. Three of us in our tent were in our sleeping bags when our fourth member Simon Oxley poked his head into the tent to tell us he was going fishing. We thought he was joking as it was now dark and had also started to rain quite heavily. How he was going to fish in the dark we didn't know as it wasn't something any of us had ever done. It must have been something Simon had done before as he seemed to be happy enough going on his own.

It was ten o'clock when Simon went and the rest of us talked for another half hour before we got our heads down. The rain was torrential now but it didn't stop us falling asleep. We were rudely awoken at quarter past eleven when Simon poked his head in the tent saying that he had got one. One of us shone a torch at his beaming face as he now produced a two to three pound trout. It was a nice fish and he wanted to tell us how he caught it but he was letting wind and rain in so we told him that he would have to wait till morning. He eventually stowed his fishing gear and waterproofs and we all got back to sleep again. At about four am we were woken again by a member of one of the other tents. Their tent had flooded and they were having to split themselves up with the rest of the tents so we had to shuffle up to let him in. It was a slow start that morning as the rain was still tipping down at nine o'clock and there wasn't much we could do until it eased off a bit, but thankfully our tent was still dry. The rain didn't stop until midday so any plans for the day that Mr Wilson had would be in doubt. Certainly there would be one tent to dry out and relocate. We were lucky it was only one tent as there was standing water everywhere.

We were so preoccupied with getting breakfast ready while trying to keep dry and generally sorting the camp out that it was about one o'clock when someone noticed that the river had risen to a level that was covering the stepping stones by at least a foot, which meant we couldn't cross the river for water and milk from the farm so we had something of a dilemma. There was a bridge downriver but it was about two miles away making it a very long walk for water. It was a big problem as the river wasn't going to go down overnight.

However, before we got too worried about our incarceration Mr Wilson was already on the case. He had brought his ropes and pulleys as he always did and had spotted a couple of trees either side of the river. So, he said we should be able to throw a rope across and make a basket to sit in and pull ourselves across. That is what we did. Mr Wilson and a couple of others went round to the other side and ropes were thrown across and secured. Then suitable pieces of wood were gathered and lashed together to form a basket making use of knots we had learned. A few hours later we had a working river crossing which of course Mr Wilson was first to test. The basket was tied to the tree so you untied the basket, stowed the rope, sat in it, lifted up your feet and you trundled out over the middle of the fast-flowing river with your toes a couple of feet above the water, then grabbing a separate rope across in front of you pulled yourself across and tied the basket up at the other side. To start with it was a bit like we were queuing up to go flying out of the tree on the first camp. We all wanted to experience being suspended over the fast-flowing river. Soon though it was a means of supplying ourselves with water, milk and eggs from the farm and it worked well. It would be about three days before the river subsided enough for us to use the stepping stones again and would be around that time that we went fishing. With Simon catching the nice trout on the first night we had high hopes of something similar, however, in the end all we could catch were salmon parr. They are a nice-looking fish that I hadn't caught before but they were all fairly small.

One evening we had all gone for a walk up to the village of Lealholm and had passed a tent that had been set up next to the track at the side of the river on our way up. We were on our way back as dusk was falling when all of a sudden up ahead we saw a big ball of flame. Immediately we all started to run towards it to see what it was. It was now a ball of smoke which rose up to reveal two boys who now started to run towards us screaming. As we neared each other we could see that most of any clothes they were wearing had burnt away. They were still smouldering as we got to them and straight away Mr Wilson ushered them into the river where we put out any smouldering clothes and bathed their burns. Then someone ran to the farm to ring for an ambulance while someone else went to get our first aid kit. Before the ambulance arrived we had covered the burns with lotion and bandaged some of them. We asked them what had happened when they calmed down a bit and they said they had a lantern hanging inside the tent and were cooking on a gas stove. The gas in the stove ran out so they unscrewed it to put a new one on, not thinking there might be some gas still left in, and the whole tent just went up in flames.

After the ambulance had been to take them to hospital we had a look at their campsite. All that was left was the stove, the lantern, cutlery and anything that was metal. There were no remains of the tent or sleeping bags at all. It was certainly an eye opener. The following day was the day we had the raft race. We spent the morning building the rafts with the race taking part mid-afternoon. Each raft had to carry four people so there were lots of ideas flying about before we finally had the finished article. No two rafts were the same ranging from oblong to triangular and time would tell if they would hold up to the challenge. The river was back to normal now and we were going to race from the far corner of the field we were in, then down and round to finish at the stepping stones. We felt it was a bit too complicated to make paddles so had opted to use poles to keep us away from the bank sides and perhaps use them as punts. It turned out the term "race" was a bit strong as there was little chance of overtaking anyone and it became one long water fight as we bumped and prodded our way along. We all made it to the finish and had great fun which is what it was all about really.

Dad and Gordon Fox on
one of the potato
picking days

Me on Brough taking him for
his exercise

Chapter 7

Malcolm had come round to the farm and we were pondering on what to do when Andrew turned up, so now there were three who had to decide what to do. As we sauntered up the stackyard I remembered that Dad had gone and bought some rabbits and had made room for them in the Nissen hut. I think they were large whites which weren't going to be pets but fattened up and sold on and he had about fifty of them. So that was our first port of call. They had red eyes and would thump their back legs down when you first went near them. It was another venture that Dad was trying out and it wasn't long before we were back in the stackyard looking for something else to do. The Vespa caught Andrew's eye and he asked if we could have a ride on it. I explained that Malcolm and I and Paul had tried a few times and it wouldn't go. He was keen even if we weren't. We explained what we had tried as he started to look it over. He lifted up the seat to reveal the petrol tank and had a look in. I said it had petrol in but he asked if there was any more we could put in, which there was.

So, after we had put some of the petrol Dad had for the lawnmower in we pushed it out into the stackyard. I showed Andrew the gears and the clutch and told him what to do when we pushed giving him the first go. We headed out of the stackyard in the direction of the railway line. The scooter is quite a weighty thing to push without it being in gear, so when the clutch is let out we could only push it about fifty yards before we had to have a breather. Our fifty yards was up and there was no sign of it starting so we had our breather. Next was Malcolm's turn so off we went again. If it was going to start now would be the time because Malcolm was the lightest and Andrew was a strong lad and we hadn't had two pushing before. We pushed it the rest of the way to the railway crossing again without the slightest sign of starting. The last run we had just done was slightly downhill and would be really hard to try and bump it off if we turned round now so I looked at the railway. Since the track had been taken up people had taken to walking down it and riding horses along it, so although the sides were still rough where the sleepers had been there was quite a good path down the middle which was nice and flat.

After another break I decided to have my go down the railway towards Foggathorpe. I selected second gear, pulled in the clutch and off we went. Then as soon as we were up to speed I let the clutch out. We went ten yards with the engine turning over, when all of a sudden it fired with a short birr and lurched forward a bit then another birr and then another, then suddenly it burst into life with a big cloud of blue smoke which enveloped Malcolm and Andrew who had now stopped pushing. I was off, the wind now racing past my ears, the scooter snaking slightly on the gravely surface. A surge of excitement went through me and I was laughing out loud. I couldn't believe we had got it going, and this feeling of sheer elation lasted another hundred yards before my eyes started to run with the force of the wind and I was finding it hard to see properly. I couldn't afford to hit the rough sides but when I slacked off the throttle the scooter seemed to snake even more, and elation turned to slight fear for a moment before I managed to slow down a bit and feel more in control. I now had the problem of what to do next as there was nowhere to turn round and the Foggathorpe road crossing was coming up in the distance. Gradually I slowed down and came to a stop making sure I kept the revs up as I didn't want it to stop this far from home. I started to try and turn it round which was really hard as I was shaking like a leaf and trying to walk it backwards and turn while straddling it and keeping the throttle going. I could see now that Malcolm and Andrew were about a mile or more away, and after a bit more shuffling and shaking I managed to turn it round. I now felt more relaxed as I got moving again and even tried a couple more bursts of speed on the way. The smiling faces of Malcolm and Andrew soon came into focus and they couldn't wait for their turn. Now we had got it going we were going to make the most of it but not on the railway, so we took it in turns to run up the farm track and back down the field until teatime brought a great afternoon to an end.

Days at junior school were coming to an end and I would be going to Market Weighton secondary school next as I hadn't passed my eleven plus. During my final year at junior school I had been picked to be head boy, which thankfully didn't entail performing too many duties, just a couple of speeches at annual events over the year. There was a summer holiday to enjoy before then with a lot of time being spent at the foulness again. We had acquired a big tractor tyre inner tube which made a good raft that we would take down there on hot days, with the rest of the time interspersed with trips, fishing and working on the farm. It was 1969 and man had landed on the moon, something that had everyone gathered round a TV to watch the momentous moment.

Another memorable moment for us around that time was getting our first colour TV and watching *Captain Horatio Hornblower* starring Gregory Peck with blue skies and blue seas, a big family moment.

We never did catch the big scary pike under the bridge but we did catch a small one which we carried back to the farm in a plastic fertiliser bag with water in. We put it in an old white stone sink that Dad had used as a trough which we had filled with water. Then we both just sat there and watched the poor thing as it remained stationary watching us, showing its teeth as it periodically opened and closed its mouth. Perhaps in some way we thought we were taming it or making it less scary. The moment however was short lived as Dad caught us and told us to take the poor thing back, which we duly did.

This would be the last summer holiday to hang out with Andrew as they were moving to Northumberland. We each still had our models of the SS *Canberra* in pride of place in our bedrooms. Andrew had already spent a year at Market Weighton school, so I already knew some of the teachers' names and a little of what to expect. My first day at Market Weighton was fast approaching and I had acquired some long black trousers and a smart blazer with a tie. The journey to school would now be by bus which we would have to catch from the junior school. I still remember the first day as we all gathered to catch the bus, laughing at each other's smart appearance and then travelling on the bus as if we were all going on some big happy holiday. The school itself was big compared to junior school with hundreds of kids meeting up again after the holidays. We all stuck together until we were ushered into the main hall where we were introduced to the teachers. There we learned which form we would be in and who would be our form teacher. I soon found that I would be in the same form as Stephen Atkinson which was great news. There were many long corridors in the school so it was a challenge just to find our form room.

Our form teacher was Mr Coumbs, the science teacher who it transpired would never be seen without wearing his white laboratory coat. We all took a seat in the room until Mr Coumbs arrived. I was sat next to Stephen and we were all jabbering away as Mr Coumbs arrived and we all went silent. He wore glasses which made his eyes look big giving him quite a stare as he looked us over. He introduced himself then quickly went into the roll call saying, "Right, let's see who we have got." The first name he called out was Stephen Atkinson to which Stephen said yes sir, then like an echo there was another yes sir. Mr Coumbs looked up and then said we will try that again shall we. Again, yes sir, yes sir. It turned out we had two Stephen Atkinsons, something that caused a laugh round the room and broke the ice and quickly brought out the friendly side of Mr Coumbs. Having the same name soon brought them together at break time. We also met his best friend who was also in our form, Mike Stephenson, and from that day on we became an inseparable foursome.

Andrew had sadly moved to Northumberland to a place called Longhorsley near Morpeth, but we had kept in touch and had arranged for me to go up and stay with them during half term. It was at least a couple of hours away by car so I was going to go by train from York and be met by Mr Macphearson and Andrew at Morpeth station. Again, this would be another big moment for me as I had never been on a train before in spite of living so close to them.

The morning of the train journey had arrived and Dad had seen me onto the right train at York and I was off with just a bottle of pop and a sandwich for company. I was quite excited about the journey and enjoyed watching the scenery go by, and then later as I made my way to the toilet being thrown from side to side as I tried to walk down the corridor. Time soon passed and it didn't seem long after I had eaten my sandwich that we were pulling into Morpeth. I grabbed my meagre bag and made my way to the exit where straightaway I saw Andrew and Mr Macphearson.

Longhorsley is only about seven miles from Morpeth so we were there in no time. It was nice to see them all again even though it hadn't been all that long since they had moved. Andrew showed me to my room. It was a big house with a big stairway and balcony round the top. It had a big bathroom and a separate toilet downstairs. I don't think I had been there half an hour before I heard Mr Macphearson tell Andrew about flushing the toilet, so I think he was losing the battle with that one. The house had a really big garden with a tennis court marked out on part of the lawn. It was by far the poshest house I had ever been in but Mr and Mrs Macphearson were nothing if not down to earth and treated me like one of the family. Andrew was still pinching some of his sleep time and going to bed late so I was more than ready for bedtime when it finally came.

Next day Ann wanted to show me her horse that she had in a stable just down the road. It was a bit bigger than Brough and wouldn't be something I would be riding as I hadn't ridden anything since my accident. We spent the morning checking out the surroundings but in the afternoon Andrew was keen to play me at tennis. I had played a couple of times at school but wasn't much of a match for Andrew.

That evening Andrew told me a couple of things that he had planned for us to do while I was there. The following day we were going swimming in a local river with some of his friends, then the day after that we would be going to climb the Cheviot, which left me with the impression that we would be going mountain climbing which concerned me a little.

The following day after breakfast we made preparations for the swimming trip. We were going there on bikes and I was going to borrow his mother's bike which hadn't had a run out for a while. So, we had to spend some time oiling it up and pumping the tyres up. Mrs Macphearson had done us a packed lunch which would go in the basket on the front of her bike along with the towels. We finally got away just before midday, Andrew on his racer and me on his mother's sit up and beg which was actually quite comfortable. The river wasn't all that far away as it turned out and we arrived just over half an hour later to a very scenic part of it. There was a fairly rapid shallow section that ran into a big pool creating a natural weir as it did so. Three of Andrew's friends were already in the river as we got there and with no one else around we had the place to ourselves. It wasn't long before we were in the water and I had been introduced to his friends. The water was about four feet deep which was ideal although it was on the cold side which we noticed less after a while. I remember commenting to Andrew that this was better than the pond at the back of his old house, to which he agreed. After a good half hour swim we climbed out to have our packed lunch. Andrew and I sat side by side and the other three sat opposite. We finished our food and drink and were sat with our legs stretched out in front of us. Andrew's three friends were doing the same so all our feet were almost together. We were chatting about this and that when I became aware of everyone behaving oddly like I'd had a joke played on me that I wasn't aware of. The other lads kept getting closer and kept lifting their feet up and were on the point of having to tell me when I finally noticed. One of Andrew's friends had six toes on each foot. His feet looked perfectly normal except he had six toes. Of course, once I had noticed they all started laughing and he wiggled his toes around all the more.

We all had another swim before we set off for home. There was no rest for me when we got back as Andrew was keen to have another game of tennis, and this time I managed to make more of a game of it as my serve improved. The rest of the evening was spent talking with his parents and Ann and catching up with events back home. It would be an early start the next morning as Andrew said we had quite a way to go.

Again, Mrs Macphearson had done a packed lunch for us and shortly after eight the following morning we were on our way. Andrew wasn't joking when he said we had a way to go, but with it being quiet country roads and nice scenery time passed quickly. It took us a good two hours to reach the place where we were going to leave our bikes to start our climb. Once there we were ready for a break so sat and had some of our food before we started our ascent.

The weather was good and I remember not being able to see any great hill or mountain in front of us. We walked up to the top of a reasonable hill only to see another, and this seemed to go on and on. Each time I thought this would be the top or at least we would be able to see the top, but every time there was another hill beyond. I think it was around two and a half hours before we finally reached the top and I don't remember seeing anyone else on the route we were taking. I can only think Andrew must have done this trip a few times before as he knew exactly where he was going, but speaking for myself and as much as I was enjoying it once would have been enough. We sat at the top and had the rest of our packed lunch before heading back down. The bike ride back seemed to be long which I suppose it would be with energy levels dropping, but Mrs Macphearson's bike held out and we got back at around six o'clock. It was only many years later that I worked out that it was an eighteen mile bike ride each way. The rest of my time there focused on tennis as my game improved and the matches became close run things making them more enjoyable. Before I knew it my time in Northumberland came to an end and I was bidding them farewell and back on the train once more.

Back home and Dad was starting to get bad back pain which was restricting some of the work he could do and was having to rely on other people more and more, but for now he was managing to keep things going. I was enjoying my time at Market Weighton school, some subjects more than others. One subject that seemed to start off on the wrong foot was French which would be taught to us by Mr Harrison. While waiting in the classroom for Mr Harrison to arrive to take us for our first lesson there was the usual noise and disarray. I was sat next to

Stephen Atkinson or "Acko" as we now called him, and during the pre-class friendly banter I tapped Stephen on the shoulder with a clenched fist. I was actually praising him and saying good lad, but at that second Mr Harrison walked in and thought it was something more and called me out to the front. The class now went quiet as I protested my innocence to no avail and was told to go to the cloakroom and fetch a size six slipper. I did as he had asked and returned with some unknown person's sandshoe.

He now told me to bend over and lift up my jacket and place my hands on his desk, which I did. Then with complete silence from the rest of the class he grabbed the sandshoe, lifted up his arm and then quickly brought it down and smacked his desk as hard as he could. I must have smarted expecting a whack on the backside, at which point the whole class erupted with laughter. He let the laughter go on just a little before holding up his arms to silence everyone before he told me to take the slipper back to where I had got it. I have to say I did see the funny side of it and was actually laughing to myself as I took the sandshoe back. When I returned to class everyone was smiling including Mr Harrison. I think he used the whole incident as some teacher class bonding event. Whether he did or not it gained him some respect and he became one of our favourite teachers, not just because of that but because of his teaching style too.

Instead of teaching boring French grammar he turned the lessons into play acting sessions. So, after we had learned a number of words and phrases we would play them out making them more complex as time went on, until he would say alright David, I want you to imagine you are driving your car down the road and then pull into the fuel station, which would be imagined by someone else from the class. I would then have to purchase fuel then drive further on and buy flowers, then go to the butchers and so on. The first time I pretended to drive a car down the classroom he stopped me to say he couldn't hear the car engine, so I had to say "Brum, Brum" as I went along. It was this kind of entertaining teaching style that made French lessons something to look forward to and taught us French at the same time. I think they managed discipline throughout the school well, like when I was caught by our geography teacher doodling on a desk with a pencil. I was told to go and see Mr Watson the woodwork teacher and get some sandpaper, then go and see the English teacher Mr Steggles who was also the deputy head teacher. I knocked on the door of Mr Watson and asked for some sandpaper which he duly got for me without asking what I wanted it for. Then I went to Mr Steggles who was taking an English class a couple of years older than me. The class was quietly working on an essay as I told him I had been sent by the geography teacher and showed him the sandpaper. He then told me to start on the first desk and sand out any pen marks I find, then move to the next desk behind that and so on until the end of the lesson. It was of course unbearably embarrassing. He didn't make me stay the whole lesson but long enough so that I didn't write on desks anymore. It was obviously something they had done before and it certainly worked on me.

Steven Atkinson 2 as I will call him lived in Londesborough and I called round to see him once on my bike. It's a really nice little village that Steven took me on a tour. We went through a lot of old woodland to arrive at a large lake which we had a walk round. The water was quite clear and I couldn't believe how many large pike we saw. I think the lake belonged to Londesborough estate and wasn't sure if it was a water we could have fished, not that I would have been keen on trying to unhook one of those large pike.

When we got to his house he showed me something he had dug up from his back garden which he kept in the garden shed. It was a complete musket with bayonet, extremely rusty of course but an impressive artifact. It would have been interesting to learn how such a thing came to be there. He showed me where he had found it which was a rough part of their garden on a slope. He said he was going to dig some more to see if anything else turned up. For now though we were going a couple of miles up the road to see Mike Stevenson who lived on a farm on the outskirts of Nunburnholme. He invited us into their living room which was unbelievably big. There was a TV in the corner surrounded by a three-piece suite and sideboard.

That took up just a quarter of the room leaving the rest of the room empty which looked really odd, but he wanted to show us a picture he had seen in a magazine of Halley's comet streaking across the sky, which it said would be visible again in 1986. It looked an amazing spectacle and one that we couldn't wait to see, however that wouldn't be for another sixteen years and when you're twelve years old that seemed like a lifetime away.

Back at school it was conker season. The game of conkers had been an annual event at junior school and was still popular at Market Weighton with a good many lads taking part. Over the years of playing conkers you would see someone with a conker that was lasting quite well, and there were all the secrets of hardening conkers by putting them in an oven or soaking them in vinegar. But in the end even the good ones eventually went the way of the rest. However, in this particular year at Market Weighton that would change. Steven Atkinson 2 had a conker that was showing promise and was beating allcomers. Normally there would be several conker fights going on at the same time during lunch break, but as Steven's conker gained notoriety and became over two hundred everyone was queuing up to pitch their conker against his to take his crown.

This went on for days. Steven said he had found it in the old wood near his house. He said it didn't look as if it was this year's as it was partly covered up and just looked old. Anyway, finally a crack appeared which had everyone at fever pitch expecting the next conker could take it and thereby taking its crown, but still it hung on till the crack finally got bigger and bits flew in all directions. There was a big roar as this king conker had fallen and lads patted the back of the victor. Then suddenly all went quiet and everyone looked in disbelief to see the kernel of the conker was still intact. The shell had gone and what was left looked like a small dried up brain with no sign of a crack in it anywhere. Steven was now laughing as he held it up for the next conker to be slaughtered, but the bell to signal the start of lessons rang saving any outcome for another day. I don't ever remember it being beat and for all I know may now have pride of place in Steven's glass cabinet.

My least favourite and weakest subject was maths but luckily Steven 2 was a whizz at it, so when we had been doing a particular type of sum all lesson and were given homework which I found out later was different to what we had been doing in class Steven 2 would show me how to do them which was more than a great help. Our woodwork teacher Mr Watson also took us for metalwork and one thing we made which we all thought was clever was a basic steam powered boat. We cut and folded tin in the shape of a boat and soldered it together, then soldered thin copper pipe which came in at the back of the boat coiled round in the centre and then went out of the back again. It all seemed very simple and we couldn't imagine how this was going to propel it through the water, but then with the help of a tank of water he showed us how. He put a small paraffin flame under the coil which heated the water in the pipe drawing it in one way and blowing it the other, which magically powered the little boats along. Of course, I couldn't' wait to show my dad as it was right up his street.

I was into my second year at Market Weighton and Mr Harrison our French teacher was now our form master. I was getting good grades and the annual teacher reports were almost embarrassingly good. I had a really good group of friends and time at school couldn't have been better.

Then one day Dad gave us devastating news which knocked us all for six. We were going to have to sell the farm. Dad had seen a specialist and was told he needed a major operation on his back and wouldn't be able to work the farm for six months, and even then it probably wouldn't be a good idea to carry on as he had. Worse was to come too as we learned they had decided to run a public house at North Dalton, as it was something Mum could run while Dad had the operation and recovered. So, as well as losing the farm we would have to change school which meant we would lose all our friends too. It was a lot to take in. I was still too young to help out in any meaningful way but I still protested that we should stay. Of course there was nothing that could be done and the farm went on the market. Slowly seeing the farm lose its animals which were its beating heart was almost too hard to bear. I think it was something Dad could see so one day he said, "Come on, we will have a look at the pub and see what you think." Nothing could take the place of the farm and everything we had here, but I had no choice but to go under duress with the rest of the family.

We arrived in the quiet village of North Dalton driving to the top of the hill and into the car park of the George and Dragon. Nothing short of another farm was going to cheer me up, so I had quite a face on as we entered the back door that led into a small kitchen. From there we went down a passage with a pantry on the right and then a sitting room at the end. Dad was already trying to drum up a bit of enthusiasm but I was determined not to like any of it. We then went through a door to stand behind the bar where we were hit with a strong smell of stale beer, which wasn't too unpleasant but a moment I remember well as I had never encountered the smell before.

Then we went into the bar where a dartboard was hung above a fireplace. It was made of plasticine, something Dad pointed out again in an attempt to get some interest going, but we were all still in a trail silently following Mum and Dad around as they went down a passage into another room where there was another dartboard, and in the corner a strange piece of furniture which was a jukebox that none of us kids had seen before. We all looked through the glass. Richard and Steven were lifted up to have a better look as Dad explained how it worked pointing out the records positioned in a big circle. Finally, there were stirrings of interest with questions from Alison and Jenny as we now made our way back to the bar where Dad opened a door. Behind it was blackness until Dad found the light switch which revealed a stairway leading down into a cellar. Now there was real excitement as we followed behind wanting to see what was round the bend at the bottom.

A room with steel beer barrels and pipework, not as mysterious as we had first thought, but not something we had seen before either. Now though as we got back to the top of the stairs the "jack in a box" was out of his box and we all went ahead of Mum and Dad to climb the stairs to the bedrooms, running from room to room then finding another flight of stairs to find two more rooms on the third floor. Six bedrooms in all meaning we could all have our own bedroom if we wanted. From the first-floor window Dad pointed out the extent of the property at the back. At the end of the car park were buildings either side of a track that led to a paddock about an acre in size with a small pond to one side. We soon made our way outside to check out the buildings. The one on the right had a passageway with a few stables coming off it. On the other side were a couple of pig sties with a covered area for them to run about. Straightaway Dad said we could get a few pigs to put in them that I could look after. I could now see that perhaps the move wouldn't be the end of the world as I had first thought. We walked to the end of the paddock where there were a couple of sheds. As we got closer I could see they were a couple of railway cargo carriages with sliding doors. So it even came with its own memento of the railway too. Now that we had seen that a move to North Dalton had things to offer it certainly helped during the final days of packing down at Waterside Farm. I had said my goodbyes to friends at school and Paul and Malcolm in the days prior to leaving. On the final day I had a chance to have one last look down at the foulness with the scary pike in his usual place under the bridge, then back at the farm I had a walk round the farm buildings with Dad to check that we hadn't left anything. The removal van had gone and it was now time for us to go too. We all got in the car and started down the farm track. I had one last look through the back window to see one of the chickens with three chicks walk into view. No doubt they would be there to greet the next owners of Waterside Farm.

Chapter 8

In 2012 my cousin Sandra was at an auction where she bought a number of books. It was sometime later when she had a chance to look at them she found four pieces of paper folded between the pages of one of the books. On closer inspection she saw that they were relating to twelve properties in the Holme upon Spalding Moor and Seaton Ross area that would be sold at auction at the George Hotel, Selby.

The date of the sale was 27th of September 1926. She then looked at the list of the lots for sale and there at the very top was Boggle House with none other than our grandad as the current tenant paying an annual rental of twelve pounds a year. She of course couldn't believe what she had found. This information she shared with me when I contacted her to ask if she had any photos of Grandad. It really is strange how the fickle finger of fate can play out sometimes.

YORKSHIRE.

EAST RIDING.

= **Particulars and Plan** =

of the

ESTCOURT ESTATE

situate in the Townships of

Holme-on-Spalding Moor and Seaton Ross,

including

12 Valuable Mixed Farms & 5 Small Accommodation

Holdings and Woodlands.

The whole extending to about

2,312 ACRES,

FOR SALE BY AUCTION,

(unless previously disposed of and in the following or such other Lots as may be

decided on) by

MESSRS. BENTLEY & SONS

at the " George " Hotel, Selby,

On Monday, the 27th September, 1926,

at 2 p.m.

Copies of these Particulars may be obtained of the Auctioneers, Knottingley;
Edwin Deavin, Esq., Estcourt Estate Office, Tetbury, Glos. or of

Messrs. Lawrence Graham & Co.,

Solicitors,

6, New Square,

Lincoln's Inn,

LONDON, W.C. 2.

GENERAL REMARKS.

Holme-on-Spalding Moor is pleasantly situate on the Selby - Market Weighton Turnpike, being 14 miles from the former and 4 miles from the latter.

The Farms on the Hotham Estate are well situate, all (except two) opening out on to good roads, and with the exception of two are in ring fences.

Each Farm is well supplied with Water from Wells and/or Ponds.

The Farms are all occupied by respectable Tenants and the majority of the Rentals have not been raised.

The majority of the Plantations are of young Oak and are very promising.

The Homesteads are all in a good state of repair and require very little expending on any of them.

The Minerals underlying the Property so far as they belong to the Vendor are reserved by him.

The growing Timber is included in the Sale.

The amounts of Owners' Drain Rate given for certain lots are the full amounts chargeable and which in some years are only charged at half or three quarters.

SUMMARY.

Lot	Description	Tenant	Area. Acres.	Rental
1	BOGGLE HOUSE and LAND	Mr J. Barker	2.700	£12
2	BACK LANE FARM	Mr C. Smart	5.149	£16
3	FARM PLANTATION	Mr. H. Finch In hand	44.546	£40
4	BUNNER END FARM PLANTATION	Messrs. T. & H. T. Stewart In hand	79.085	£78 16s 0d
5	ARGLAM LANE FARM	Mr W. Raper	21.865	£25
6	OAKS FARM	Mr W. Jibson	32.897	£38
7	LINCOLN PLATTS FARM in SEATON ROSS	Mr. J. H. Sprsley	231.859	£180
8	ARGLAM FARM PLANTATION	Mr. C. W. West In hand	241.747	£110
9	WELHAM BRIDGE FARM (WEST)	Mr. R. A. Loverack	98.978	£119
10	WELHAM BRIDGE FARM	Mr A. W. Haworth	204.419	£210
11	BURSEA LANE END FARM PLANTATIONS	Messrs. H. Smith In hand	145.282	£79 10s 0d
12	BURSEA FARM	Mr. F. S. Harrison	88.262	£78
13	EAST BURSEA FARM	Mr. H. Harnsby	191.434	£154
14	HASHOLME HALL FARM PLANTATION	Mr W. Brown In hand	412.635	£360
15	HASHOLME GRANGE	Mr. A. Williamson	398.348	£377 10s 0d
16	HASHOLME GARTH FARM	Mr. A. Williamson	198.198	£84
17	HASHOLME CARR FARM	Mr. J. Heath	138.044	£81

TOTAL A 2,803.608 £1,770 16s 0d

The Brick-built DWELLING HOUSE

known as

BOGGLE HOUSE

with the range of Outbuildings comprising:—Stable, Loose Box and Piggery and etc.

CLOSE OF ARABLE LAND

adjoining being Nos. Pt. 1065 and 1065, extending to a total area of 3.756 ACRES, situate in Moor End Road, HOLME-ON-SPALDING MOOR, let to Mr Joseph Butler, on an Annual Tenancy at a Rental of £12.

NOTE.—The Wood residues are the Property of the Tenant.

The first time I had a chance to return to Waterside Farm was at the age of seventeen after I had passed my driving test. I didn't want to drive down the lane to the farm and impose on the owners, so I chose to park on Holly Lane and walk to the rear of the farm via the railway. There I encountered an industrial style eight feet high iron fence which encompassed the rear of the property. I couldn't understand why they felt the need to erect such a thing. As I walked along the old railway I could see the triangular field that I had ploughed eight years previously through the fence as I walked along. They weren't growing any crops in it and it soon became evident they were using the field as a tip with what looked like hundreds of tons of soil and rubble heaped up on it. Sadly I had seen enough so I decided to walk down to the foulness.

Straightaway I could see the bridge had been altered. Instead of the wooden vertical rails at the side they were now metal rails splayed out at an angle which I guess would be to let bigger machinery get across. Once on the bridge the first thing I wanted to know was if there was a pike under the bridge. The metal rails were too far away to lean on so I had to kneel down to have a look and there in the usual place was a pike, probably not the same one as it looked smaller but a pike nonetheless which put a smile on my face as I watched it for some time. On my way back I started to walk across the old railway crossing where I was met by a lad on a bike. I said hi there as I stopped to let him pass, then this lad that I didn't recognise said, "Alright, Dave, how are you?" The voice was familiar but I didn't know who it was. "It's Stephen," he said, "Stephen Atkinson." I was dumbstruck, this wasn't the Fatty Acko I had known five years previously, this lad was slim and tall. I couldn't believe it. It took some time to pick up on some of his traits, such as the way he laughed and smiled. The more I said that I couldn't' believe it the more he laughed. It was of course great to see him and we spent a good while catching up on times past.

Over the following forty odd years I have kept in touch with the Ross family and periodically call in for a visit. I have also from time to time caught up with Paul who still lived in Holme upon Spalding Moor, but more recently has moved back to his childhood home after his mother died. On a recent visit he told me that Waterside Farm had been empty for the past three years which caught my attention. I said it would be great to have a look around so he told me who owned it and where he lived. I told my brothers and sisters what I had found out and they were all keen on having a look round if we could get permission.

A few weeks later my brother Steven had to visit Holme upon Spalding Moor on business and took the opportunity to call on the owner to see if it was possible for us to have a look round. The owner kindly said we could but pointed out that the property was now in a poor state of repair and we must take care if we went into the farmhouse. My brother couldn't wait to tell me the news and it wasn't long before we arranged for us all to go down for a look. It sounded as if the farm would soon be pulled down so this may be our last chance to see the old place.

On the day of our reconnection with the farm there was of course an air of excitement which strangely turned to slight apprehension. We travelled down in three cars so decided to park down Holly Lane and then walk across part of a stubble field into the stackyard. The farmhouse from the front didn't look too bad; previous owners had at some point lifted up the sloping roof to give more headroom in the bathroom and bedroom. They had also built a new and bigger veranda. The veranda door was locked so we walked round to the front. Both of the stables at the sides had been knocked down and they had built a single-story extension off the old living room. It was this extension that was showing signs of collapse, but the door here was unlocked so we carefully made our way in.

There was a real buzz as we made our way into the old living room which was pretty much the same except they had made a big feature of the fireplace. The reception room was just the same and straightaway we reminisced about the card games that we had played there. The kitchen and dining room were the same too and the stairs were now open plan. We were now all chipping in with memories, Brandy's bed used to be here, Dad used to fall asleep in his chair there, and the meat hooks used to be here.

We now climbed the stairs and it was here that the deterioration could really be seen. The floor in my old bedroom had gone and all the ceilings were down exposing the rafters of the roof, but what had been the girls' room and Mum and Dad's looked just as they were. Richard and Steven were now standing in the room where they were born. It was all a bit surreal and amazing how some old bricks and mortar could bring back such vivid memories. We now spent about twenty minutes taking photos and retracing our steps, each of us now in our own thoughts. Dad had been gone twenty years or more now but I couldn't help but wonder what he would've made of the occasion. We now slowly made our way out making sure we hadn't missed anything. The parameters of the garden had changed but I could still see the spot at the other side of the dyke where I had first met Paul Simpson.

The Dutch barn had gone as had the chicken hut. The Nissen hut was a pile of broken breeze blocks where it had once stood, but the main barn and adjoining building where we had kept the calves and the pigs were still there. Inside the main barn most of the pigpen walls had gone but we could still identify the area where we would watch Dad mix the meal.

Then as we went into the adjoining building where we had kept the calves memories of the noisy trip in the Bedford van to pick them up came flooding back. Once outside again we spent some time identifying areas where various events happened, like where I had fallen off Brough and where various old photos had been taken, particularly where Richard and Steven had been photographed on their bike with bowls on their heads as helmets. Rain was forecast so before it arrived we decided to have a walk over the railway to the foulness. Walking over the old railway made me feel old as forty feet high mature oak trees now grew where I had once walked with Grandad to collect coal. The walk and the view down to the river was just the same but the bridge had changed again. It was now a big new concrete one with iron railings. As we neared the bridge we were talking about the time when Richard had fallen in and had to be quickly dragged out. Then as we all made our way to the middle of the bridge there was stunned silence. Where once the twenty feet wide, three feet deep foulness had run, with shoals of three quarter pound roach and silver dace in the distance and monster pike under its bridge, now had a three feet wide, one foot deep flow of brown weedy water flowing beneath. Where once we had paddled along on an inflated tractor inner tube now barely had enough open water for a duck to land on. It really was sad to see. There was no sign of fish of any kind though I'm sure the odd eel and bullhead would lurk somewhere. The scary pike of yesteryear would have found it slim pickings and would barely have had enough room to turn around. It was something of a sad end to our visit but we were all pleased we had come to transport ourselves back to the Waterside Farm of the 1960s one last time.

Waterside Farm lives on

A view of the front of the farm today with the more recent extension showing a greater state of collapse.

A view of the foulness today looking down stream from the bridge, this used to be fifteen feet wide and three foot deep. The place where Dad would trot a line down for the big roach and Dace.

A view of the rear of the farm where long before the extension, Dad had been fixing the roof

A view looking upstream from the bridge today, the place where the big scary pike sped off to safety after out failed attempt to catch him.

A view of the railway today where we pushed the carriage and the scooter burst into life. Mature oak trees now grow where I once picked coal with Grandad

Steven & Richard on their bike, a half-hearted recreation of the Steven & Richard bike photo

All of us outside the main barn one last time.

Left to right, me, Alison, Richard, Jenny & Steven

Printed in Great Britain
by Amazon

79957556R00071